One Saturday —in 82 on— Broadway Market

STUART GOODMAN

First published in the United Kingdom by:
OWN IT! Entertainment Ltd
Company Registration Number: 09154978

Cover Photography: Stuart Goodman

Design: Caroline Lee

ISBN: 9781916052338

WWW.OWNIT.LONDON

My dad was born in Berwick Street market in 1916.
My grandmother sold loose cigarettes there.
Perhaps it runs in the family.

Introduction

I first found the market by mistake in 1976. It's a long sad story involving my friend Rob's bladder and my car's braking system. As I said, it was a long sad story.

I fell in love with the place; the cobbles, the people, the Cat and Mutton pub. Another mate and I were looking for a place to use for a screenprinting venture. Thus was born HotShots, a thankfully short-lived extravaganza at number 27.

By the end of 1977, I lived in the market in an exceptionally squalid flat above and below number 52. I met both my wives there, though mercifully not at the same time.

These photographs were taken one Saturday morning in March 1982, for a Greater London Council exhibition at the Royal Festival Hall. Ironic really, because the GLC had a compulsory purchase scheme for a nightmare version of Westway through East London, which included the Broadway.

One morning I saw a bloke with a clipboard measuring the shops opposite. "This for the refurbishment?" I asked him innocently. "No mate, it's for the demolition". Stephen Selby, later famously described in a Guardian piece as "not a bohemian" and I set up the Broadway Market Preservation Society that evening in the Cat and Mutton. This, and its successor the Action Group led the protests against the proposals. I ended up as chair of both groups.

We had huge support both from the traders and the local residents. In 1978 we organised a street festival and decorated the market with homemade bunting. It rained. It rained so hard the majorettes looked like they were choreographed by Busby Berkeley.

Stephen was last seen riding off in a horse and cart with the deputy leader of the GLC and local politicians. To this day he insists it was a horse and carriage. All I know is it had a horse at one end and wheels at the other. The bands sought refuge in the Cat and Mutton. It was a good day, we were assured. I remember the hangover.

We also had an exhibition of photographs of

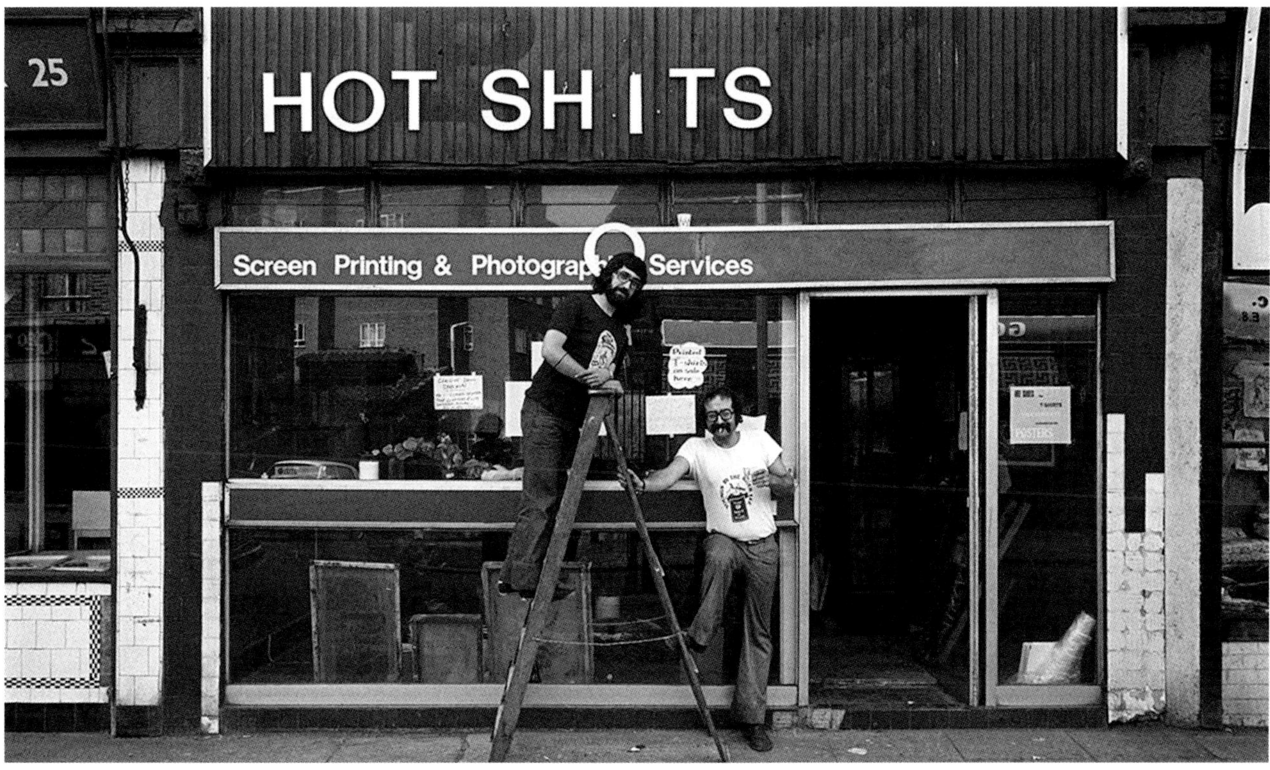

HotShots, June 1977, with Keith up the ladder and me with my feet on the ground. **Photo: Geoff Howard.**

market shopkeepers, specially taken by Geoff Howard and sponsored by Express Newspapers. Well, sort of. I nicked the film from them. Stephen had spent weeks in the Hackney Library archives gathering old pictures of the market. These were displayed with Geoff's photos in London Fields School.

Geoff's photos were later published in the British Journal of Photography and Israel Renson, the celebrated local historian, wrote a booklet for us called 'Up the Broadway'.

What the festival achieved was to make the community aware of its own strength. We had regular meetings at Hackney Town Hall and County Hall. The Hackney Gazette was truly unwavering in its support. Sir Geoffrey Howe was even persuaded to venture into deepest Hackney to meet us. For the life of me I cannot remember why. Our local MPs, Margaret Morgan and then Ron Brown were very involved.

I moved away. Stephen and some of the others did not. He went on to establish the Off Broadway gallery and later the bar of the same name with his son. When these photos were taken, Off Broadway was a hole in the ground.

So, this was a day in the life of Broadway Market. More like half a day and not quite half a market. Half a dozen stalls and not many more customers. To say it was dead on its feet would have been optimistic. Miracles happen. The market survived just, and much later, with the intervention of the new Broadway Market Residents and Traders Association, flourished and blossomed. I found the negatives. The result is this book.

I'd like it to be my heartfelt thanks and tribute to those who worked so hard to keep the market alive. Some of the people, very sadly, are not.

I miss the place. Not the squalor, the outside loo, the wasp's nest, the cold… but the people, the community and somehow, the optimism. There wasn't a gastro pub in sight and who had ever encountered a buffalo burger?

Stuart Goodman

Footnote

While a student in Swansea in the late '60s, I had directed 'A Man for all Seasons', a brilliant play about the life and death of Sir Thomas More. I recently read that More's daughter Margaret had lodged in a house on London Fields, she had walked through the Broadway and over the Cat and Shoulder of Mutton Bridge, carrying his food to the Tower of London in the days before his execution.

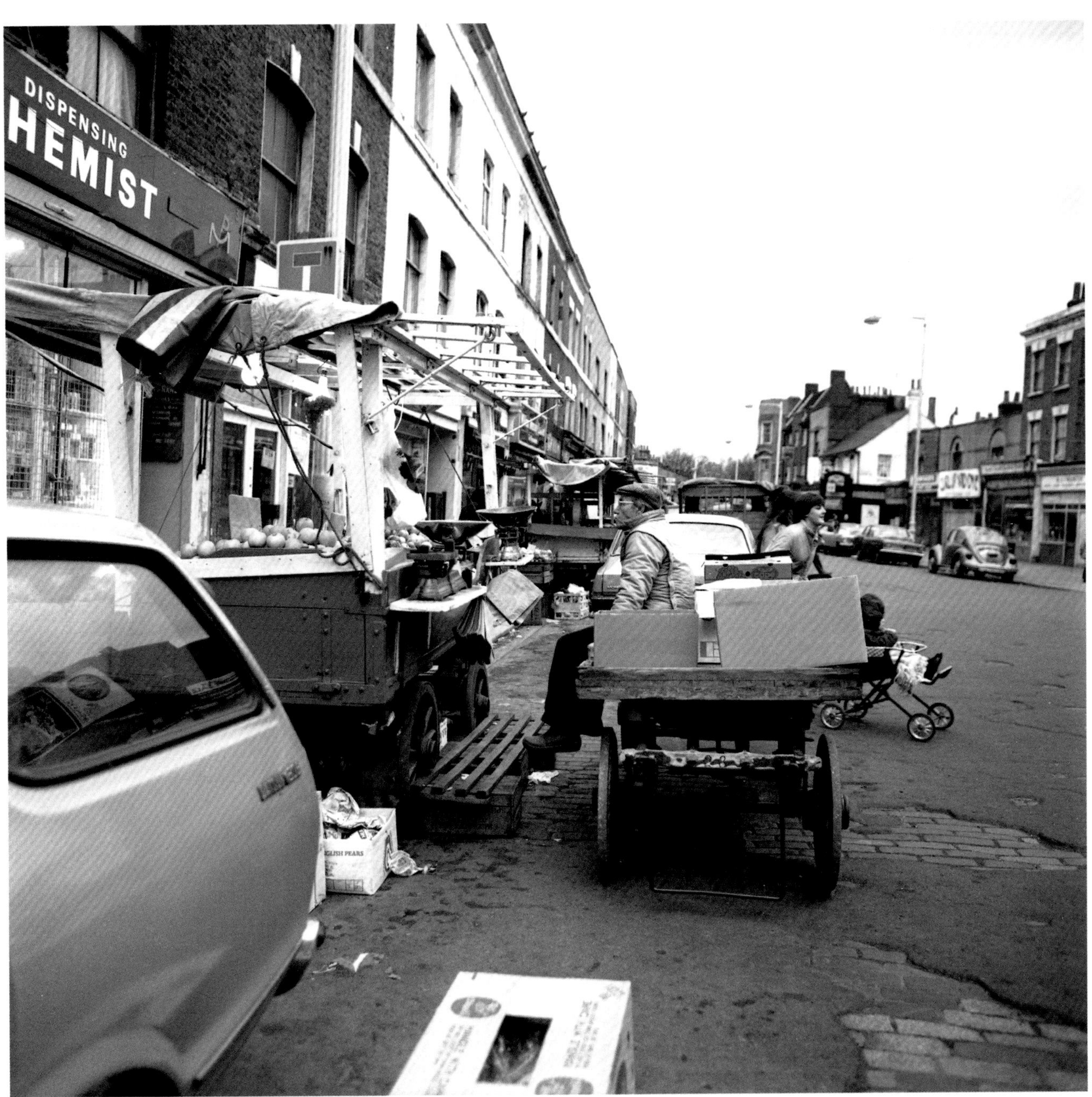
DISPENSING
HEMIST

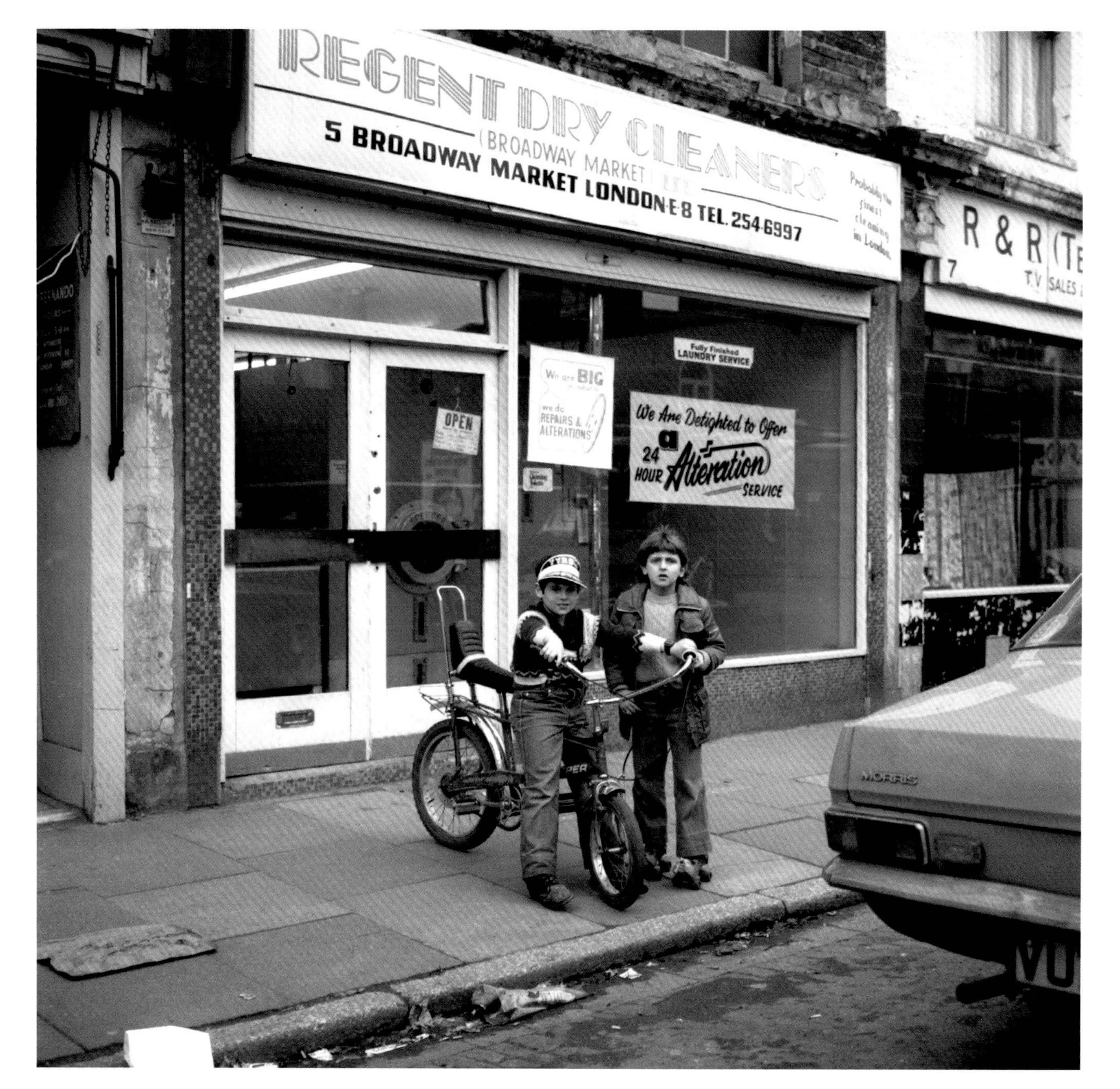
REGENT DRY CLEANERS
(BROADWAY MARKET)
5 BROADWAY MARKET LONDON E 8 TEL. 254 6997
Probably the finest cleaning in London.
R & R
7
T.V SALES
Fully Finished LAUNDRY SERVICE
We are BIG
we do REPAIRS & ALTERATIONS
OPEN
We Are Delighted to Offer
a 24 HOUR Alteration SERVICE
MORRIS

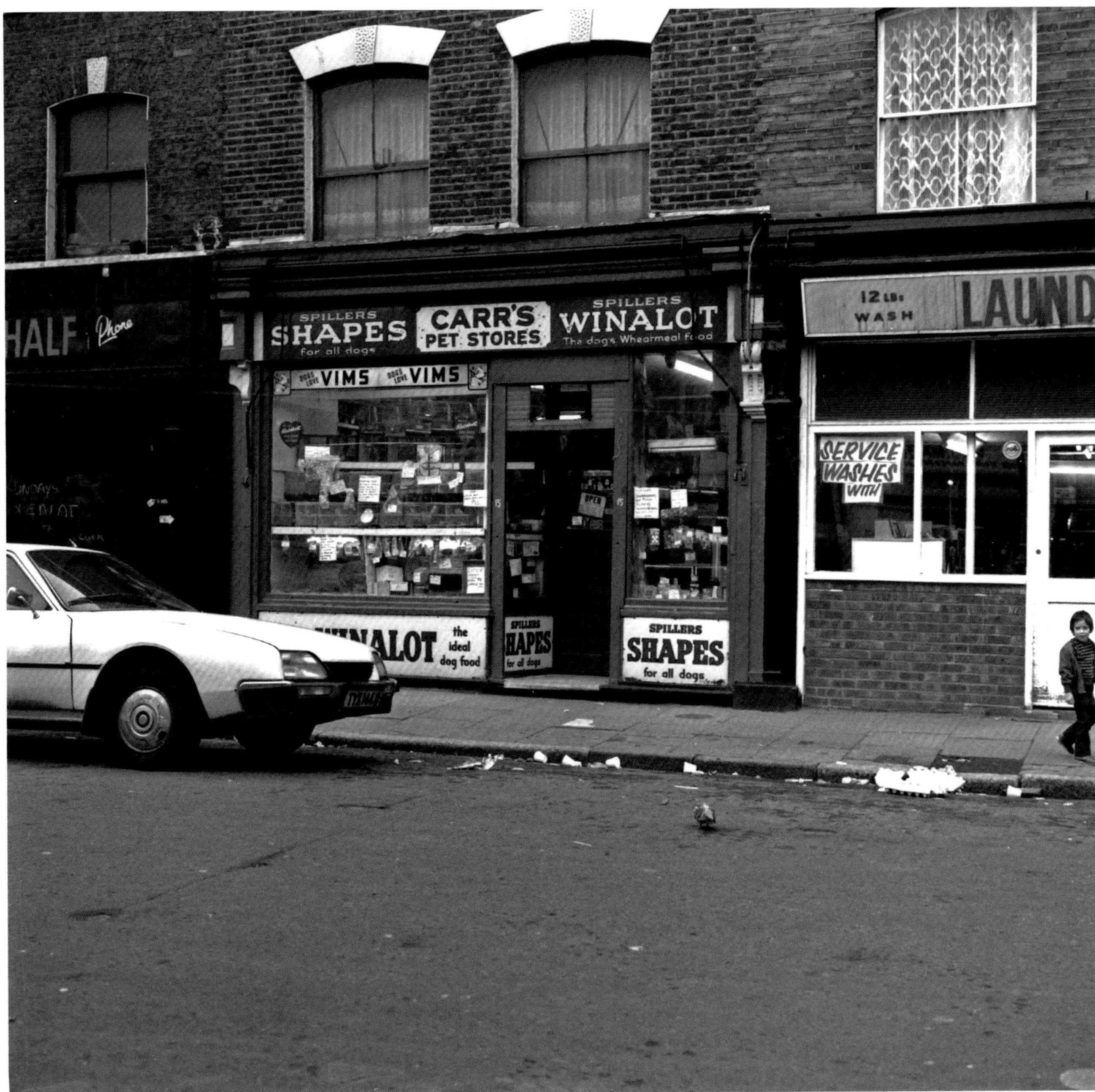
SPILLERS
SHAPES
for all dogs
CARR'S
PET STORES
SPILLERS
WINALOT
The dog's Whearmeal food
DOGS LOVE VIMS
DOGS LOVE VIMS
WINALOT
the ideal dog food
SPILLERS
SHAPES
for all dogs
SPILLERS
SHAPES
for all dogs
12 LBs
WASH
LAUND
SERVICE
WASHES
WITH
HALF
Phone
OPEN

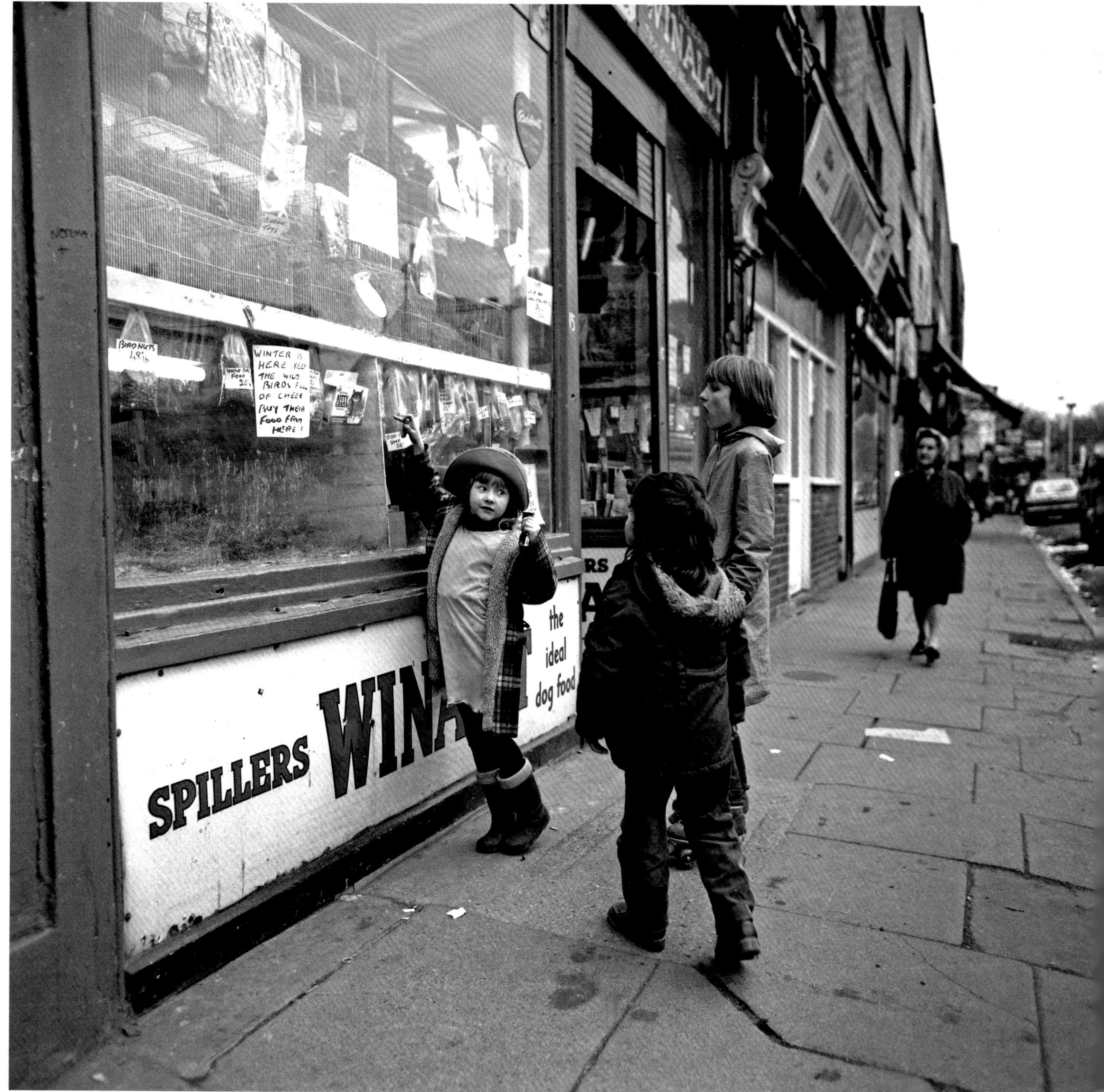
WINALOT
WINTER IS HERE KEEP THE WILD BIRDS FULL OF CHEER BUY THEIR FOOD FROM HERE!
BIRD NUTS
SPILLERS
WINA
the ideal dog food

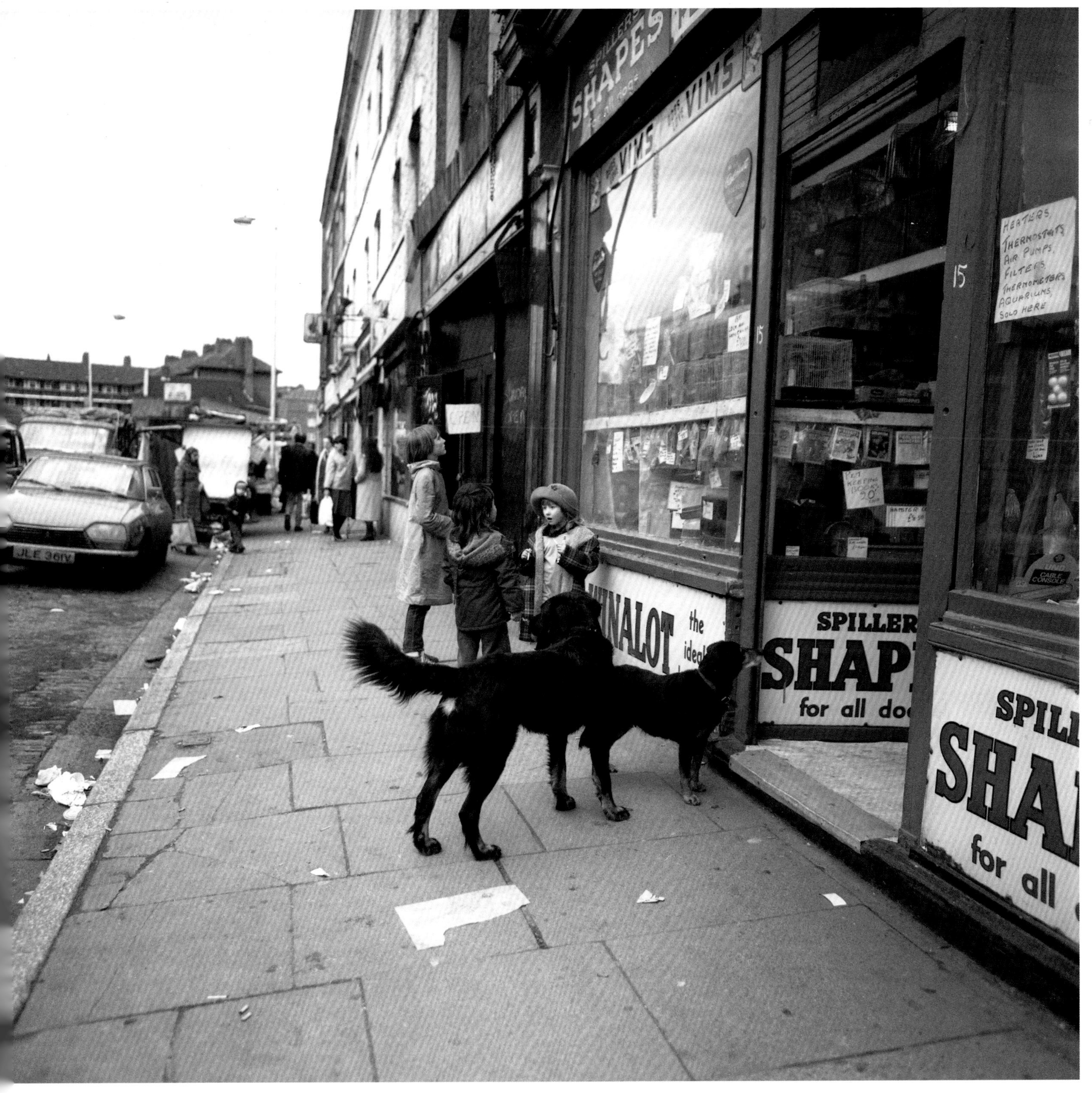
SPILLERS
SHAPES
VIMS
VIMS
HEATERS,
THERMOSTATS,
AIR PUMPS,
FILTERS,
THERMOMETERS,
AQUARIUMS,
SOLD HERE
15
15
OPEN
JLE 361V
INALOT the ideal
SPILLER
SHAP
for all do
SPILL
SHA
for all
CABLE CONSOLE

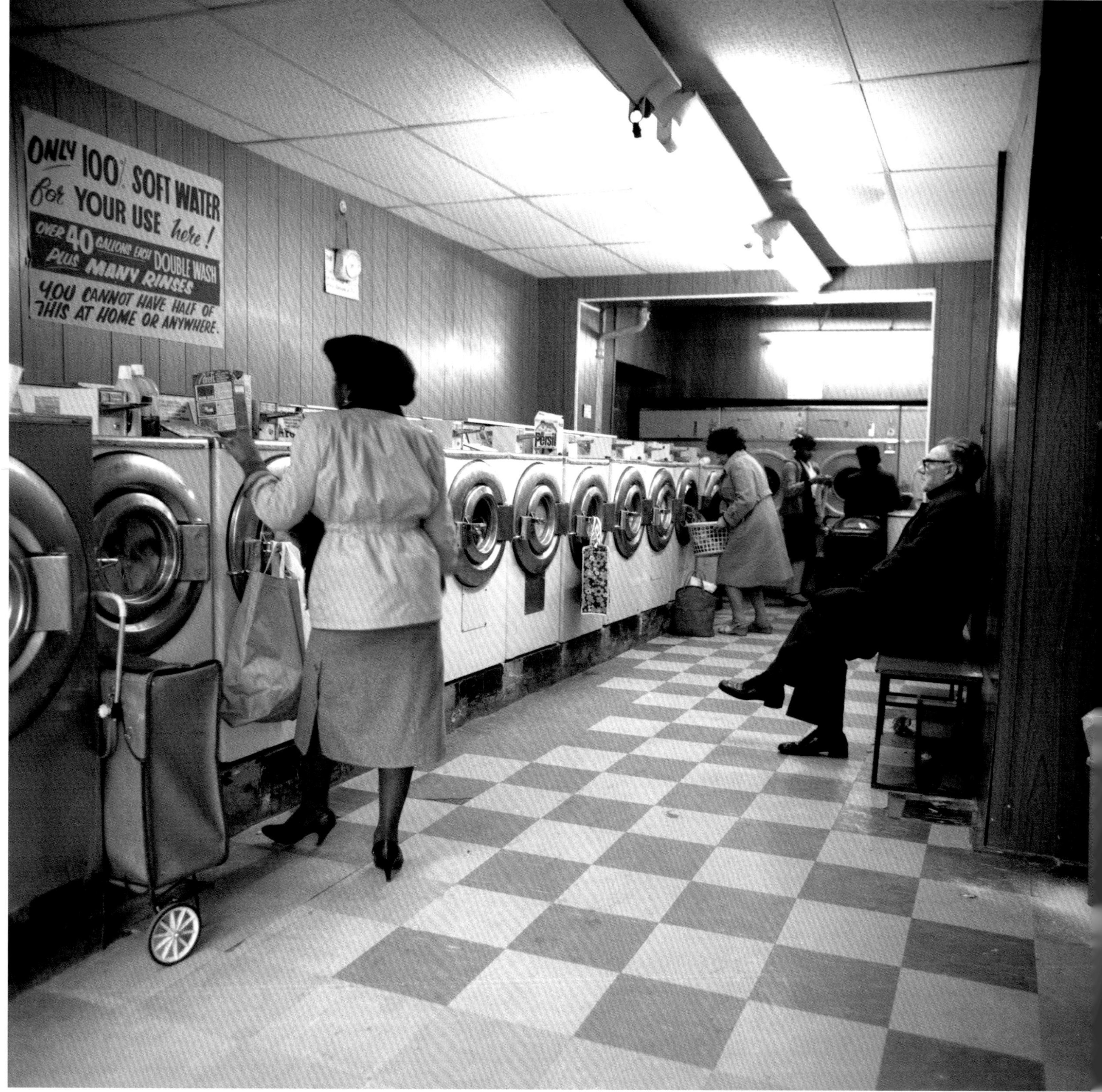
ONLY 100% SOFT WATER
for YOUR USE here!
OVER 40 GALLONS EACH DOUBLE WASH
PLUS MANY RINSES
YOU CANNOT HAVE HALF OF
THIS AT HOME OR ANYWHERE.
Persil

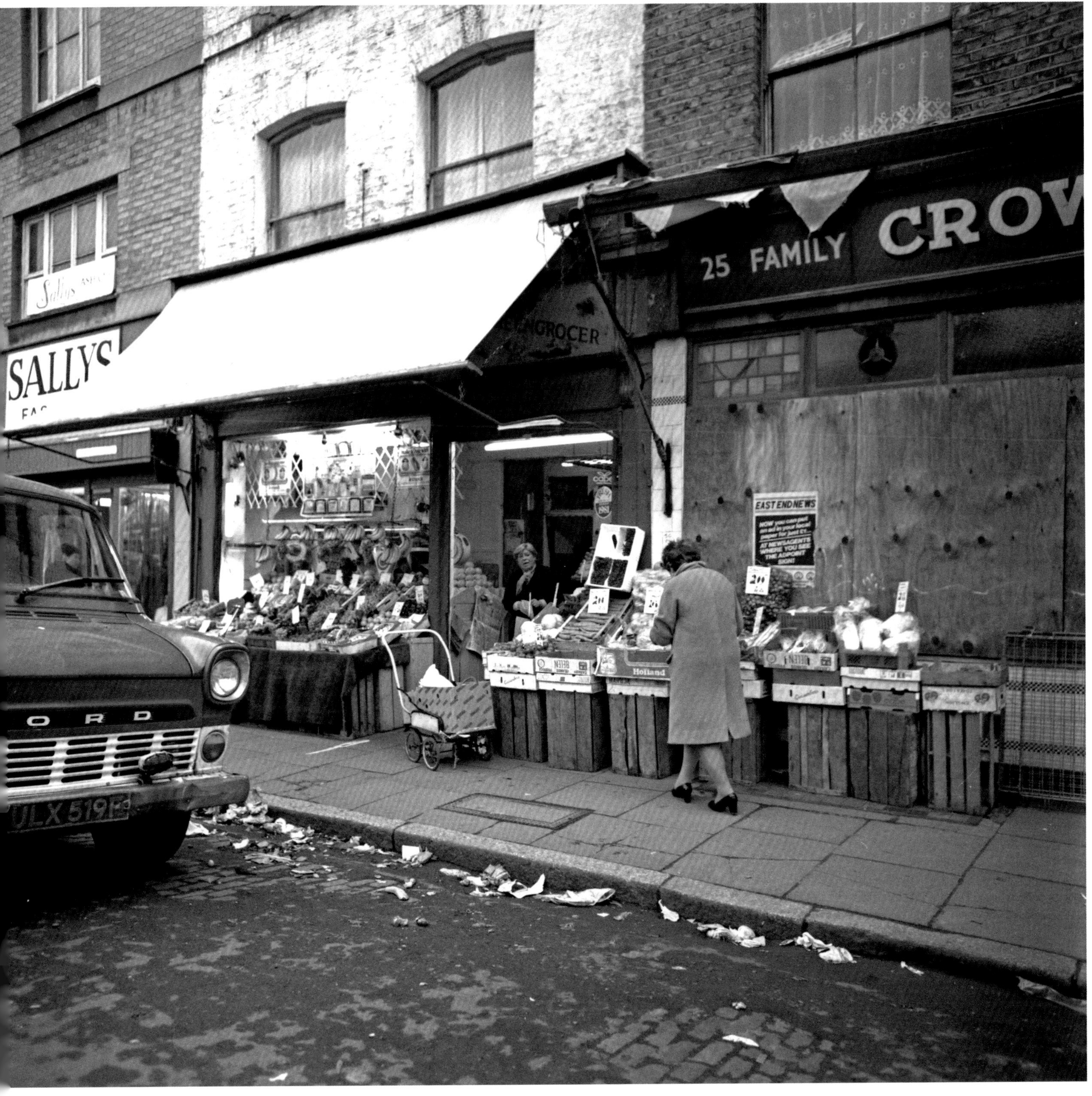

SALLYS
25 FAMILY
CROW
GROCER
EAST END NEWS
ORD
ULX 519F
Holland

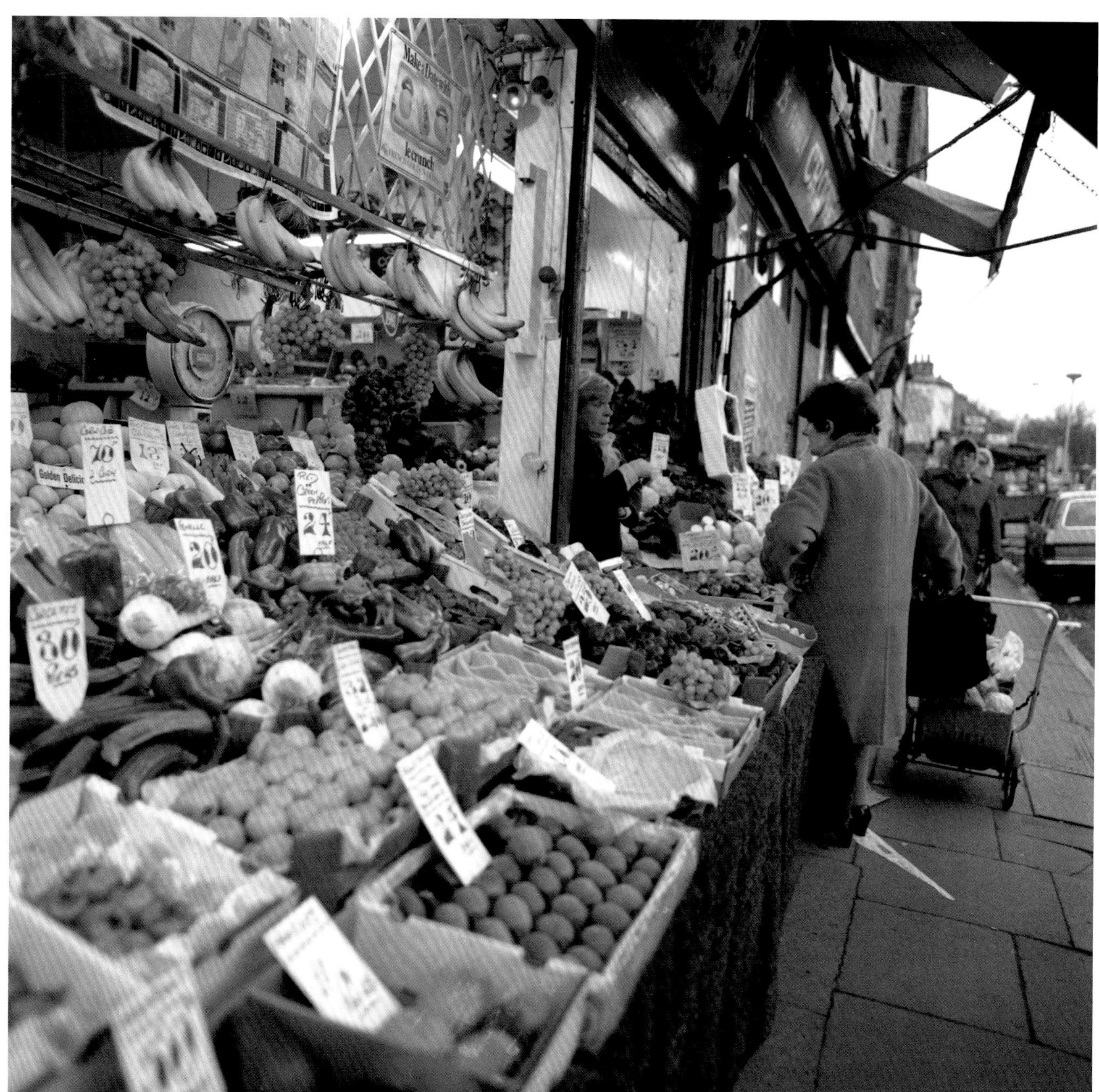
Make a Date with
le crunch
Golden Delicio
70
24
20
30

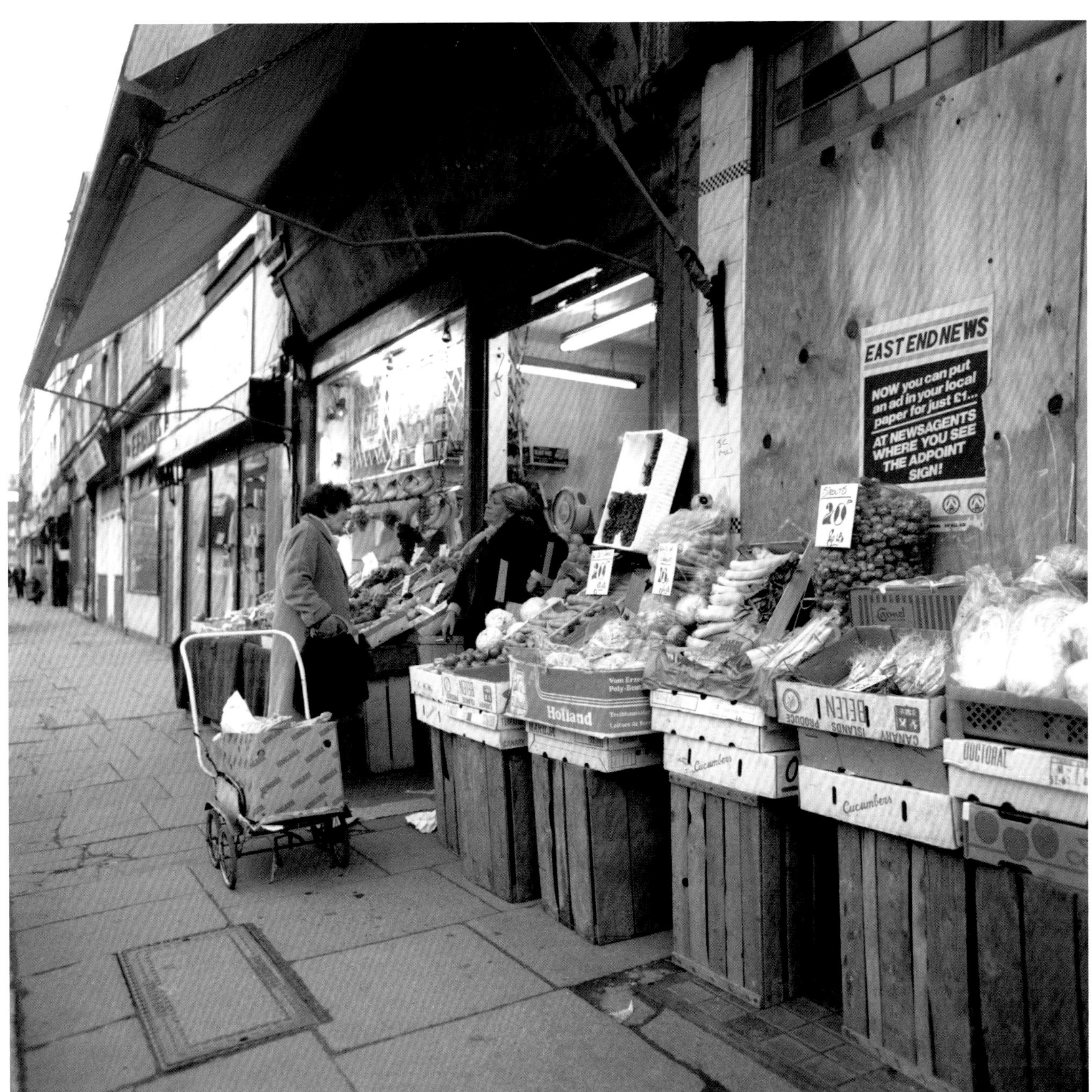
EAST END NEWS
NOW you can put an ad in your local paper for just £1...
AT NEWSAGENTS WHERE YOU SEE THE ADPOINT SIGN!
Holland
Cucumbers
Cucumbers

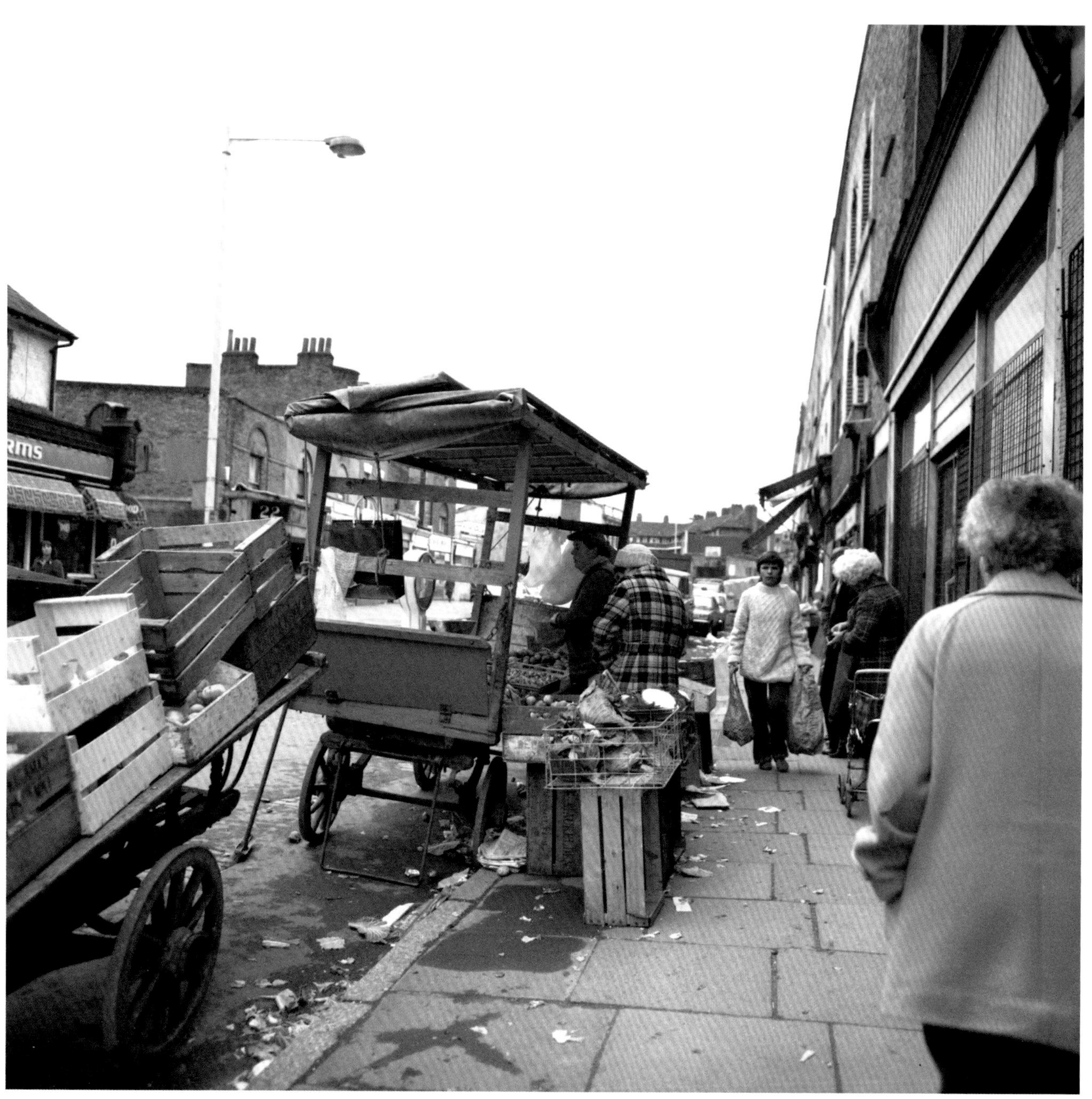

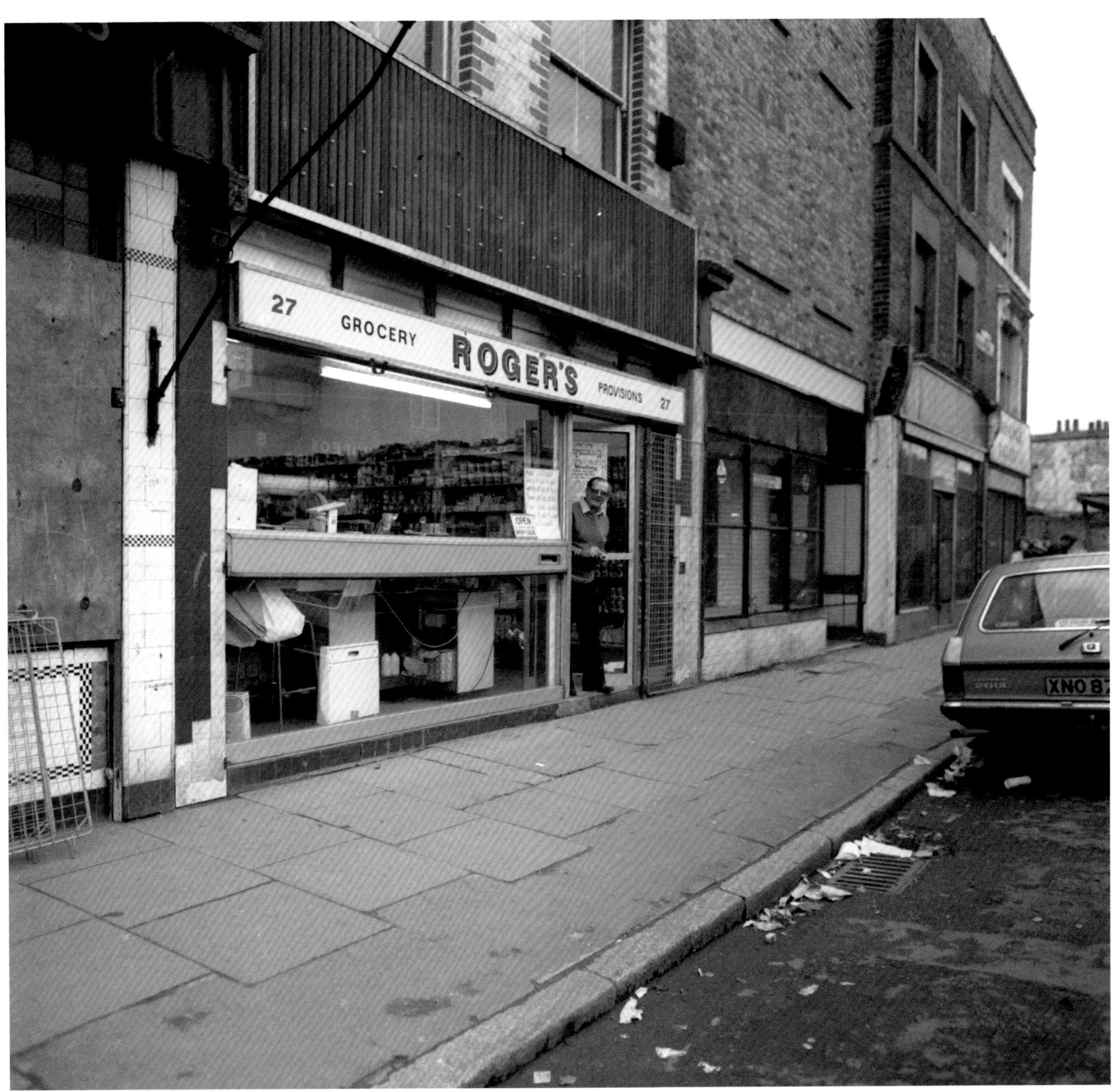
27
GROCERY
ROGER'S
PROVISIONS
27
OPEN

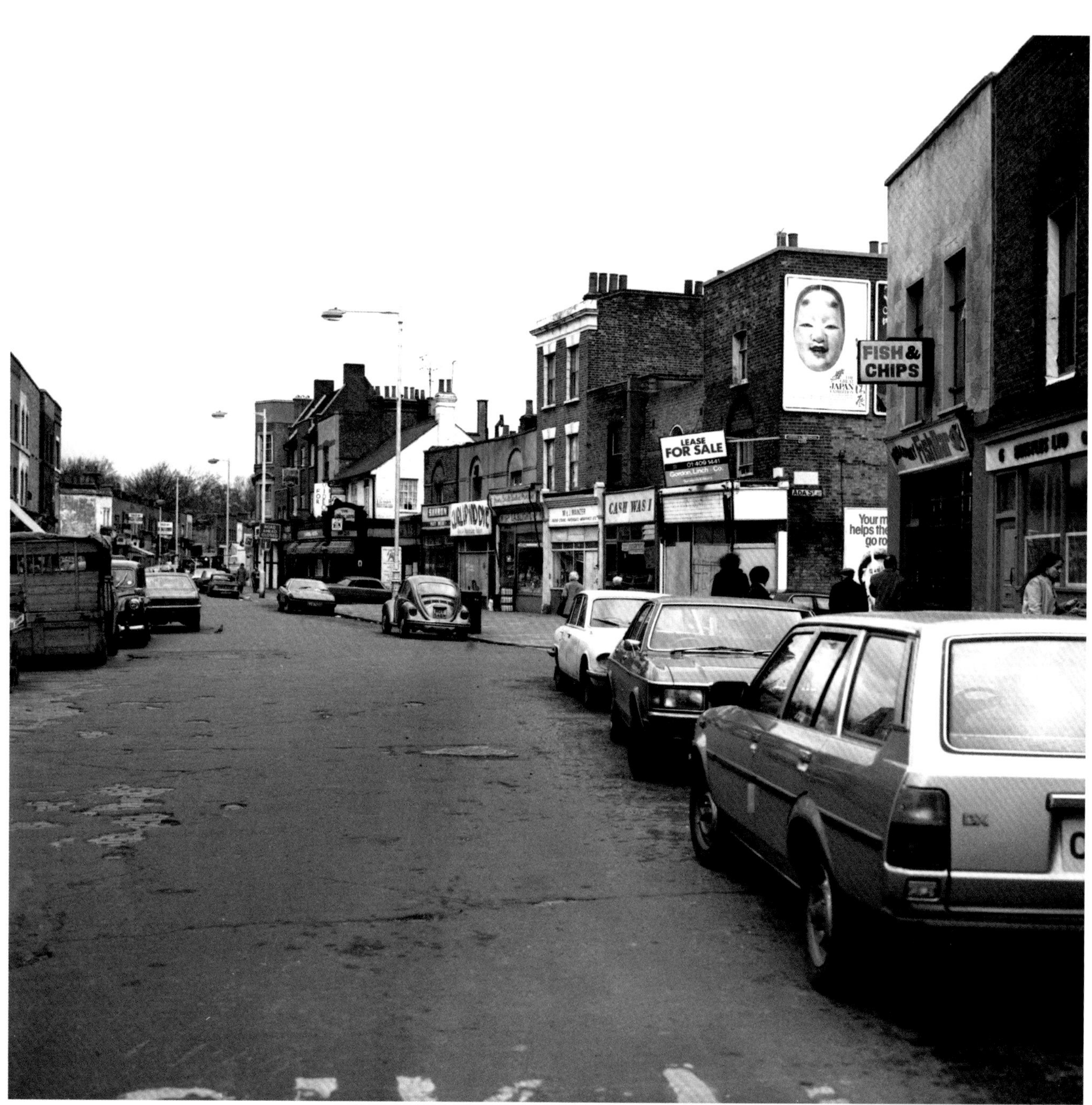
FISH & CHIPS
LEASE
FOR SALE

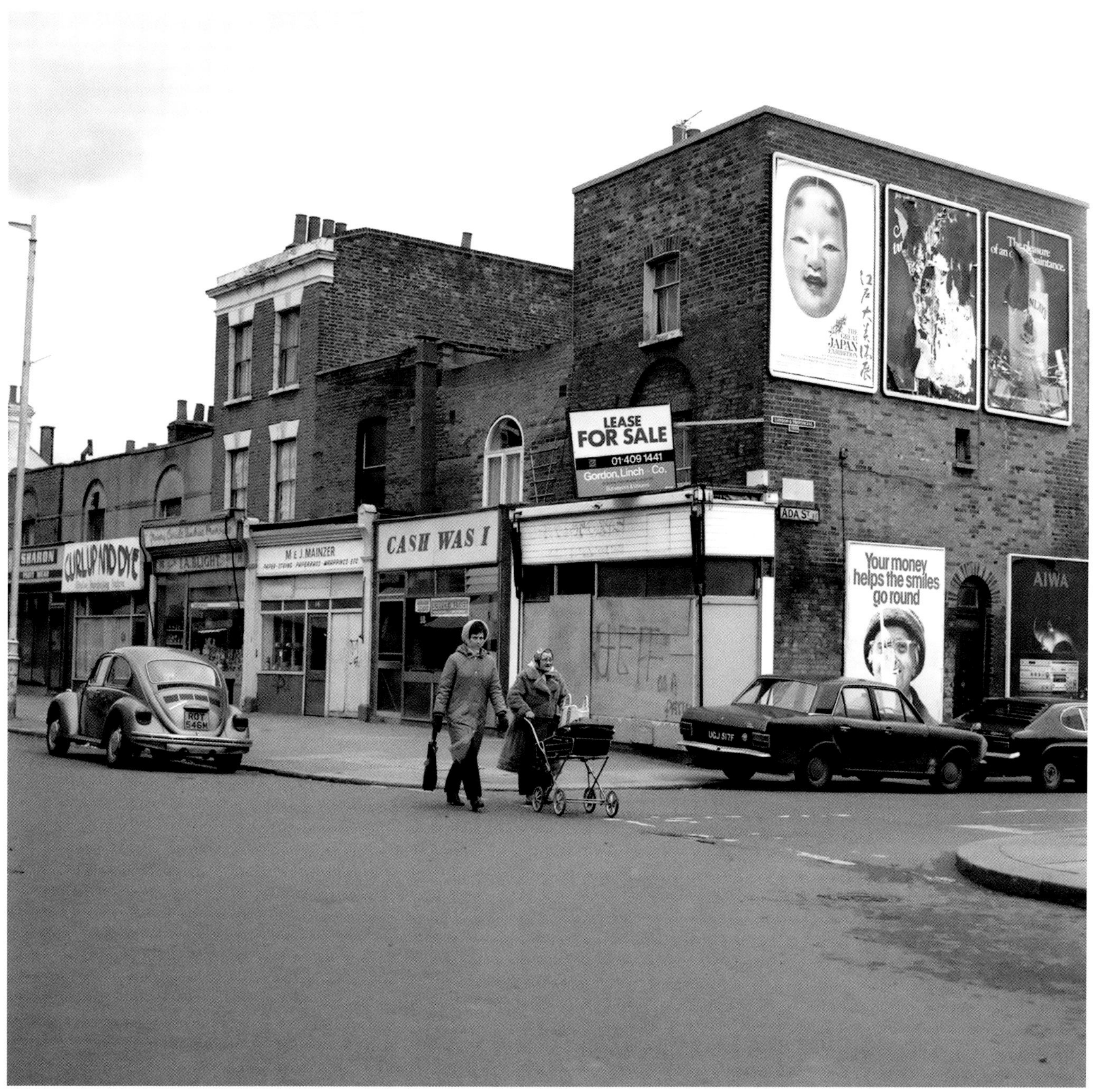
SHARON
CURL UP AND DYE
M & J. MAINZER
CASH WAS I
LEASE
FOR SALE
01-409 1441
Gordon, Linch Co.
THE GREAT JAPAN EXHIBITION
ADA ST
Your money helps the smiles go round
AIWA
ROT 546M
UCJ 517F

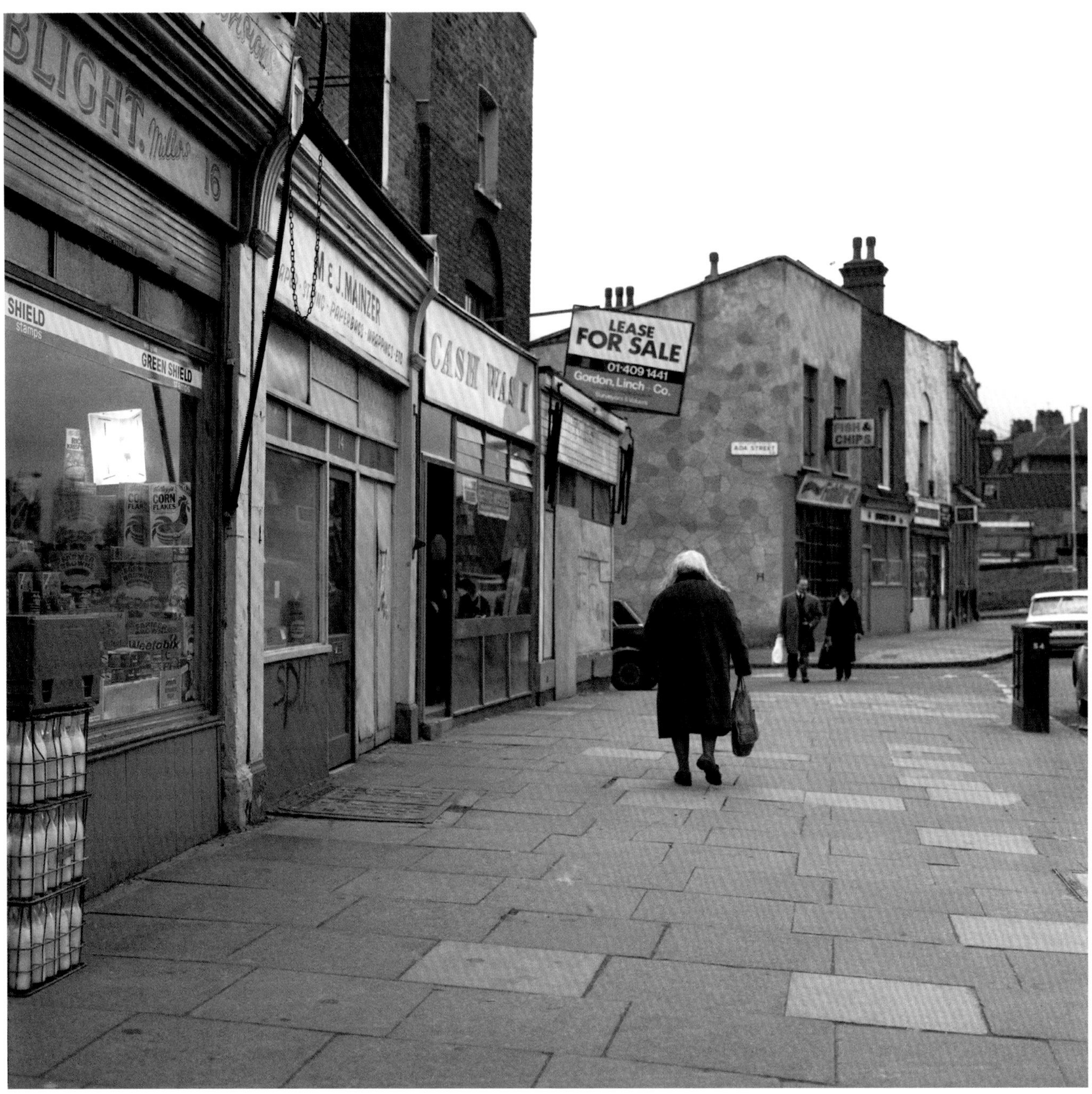
BLIGHT.
16
SHIELD
stamps
GREEN SHIELD
CORN FLAKES
M & J. MAINZER
CASH WASH
LEASE
FOR SALE
01-409 1441
Gordon, Linch - Co.
ADA STREET
FISH & CHIPS

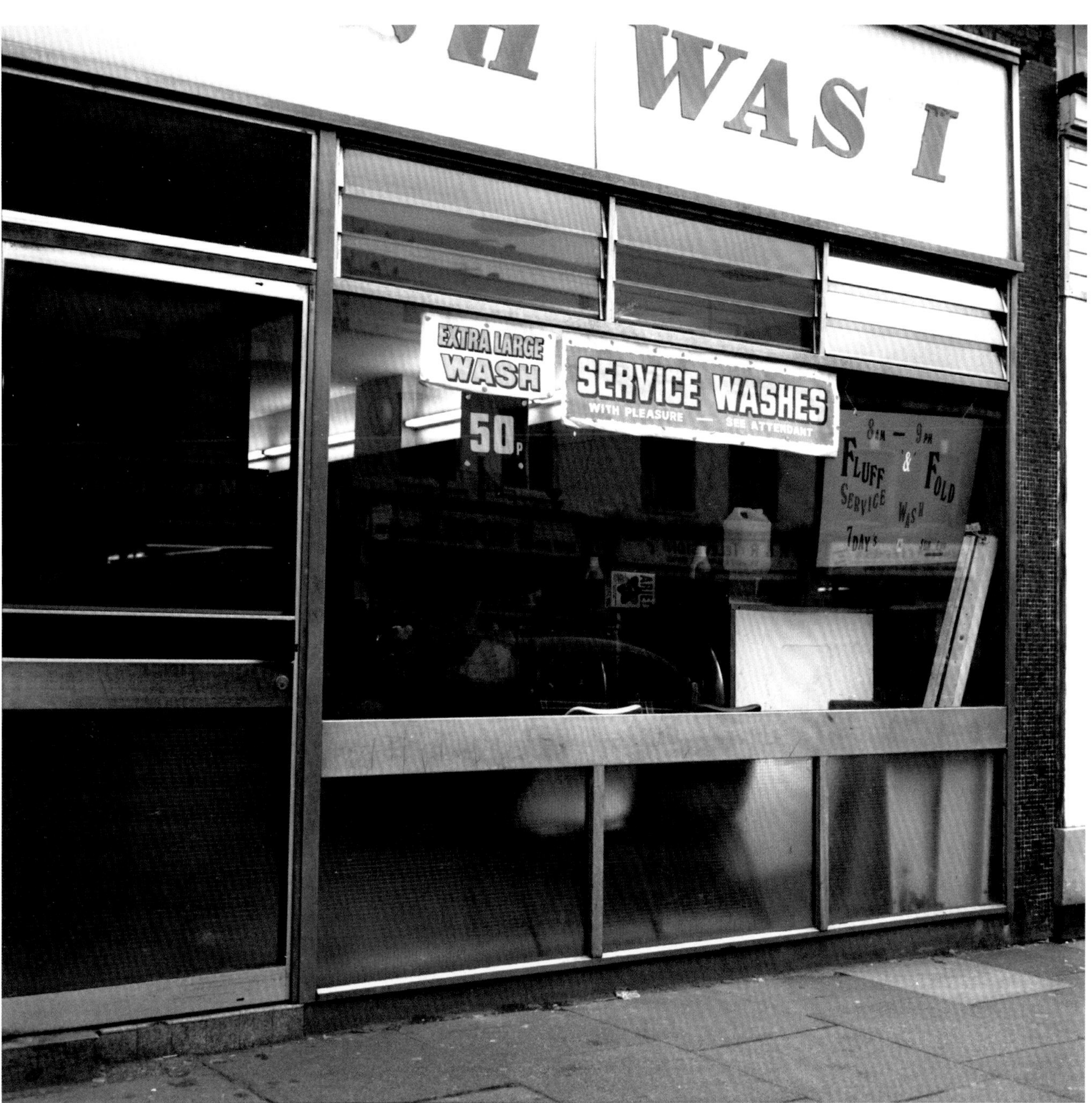

H WAS I
EXTRA LARGE WASH
SERVICE WASHES
WITH PLEASURE — SEE ATTENDANT
50p
8AM – 9PM
FLUFF & FOLD
SERVICE WASH
7DAYS

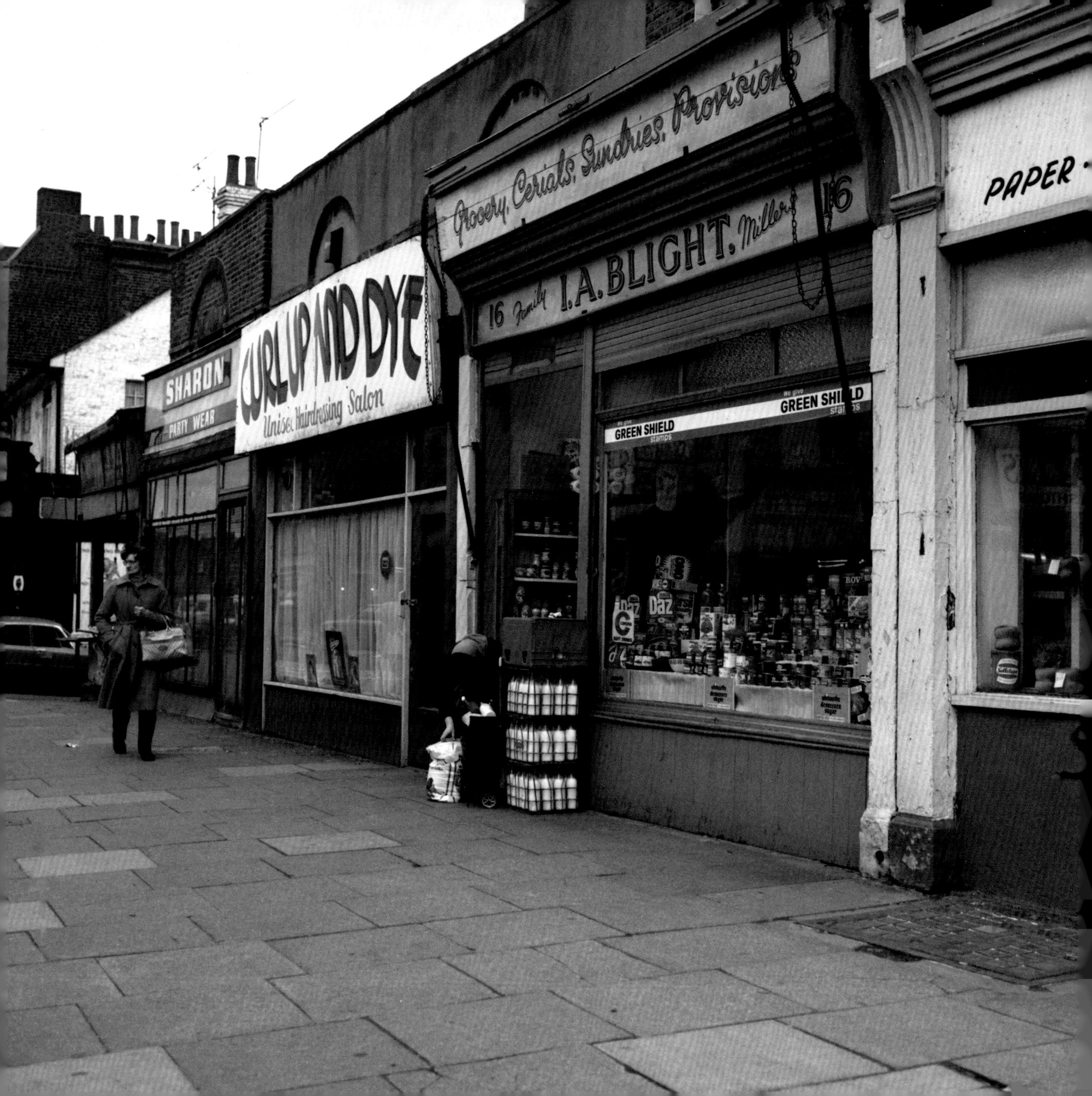
Grocery, Cerials, Sundries, Provisions
16 Family I. A. BLIGHT. Miller. 16
PAPER
CURL UP AND DYE
Unisex Hairdressing Salon
SHARON
PARTY WEAR
we give
GREEN SHIELD
stamps
Daz

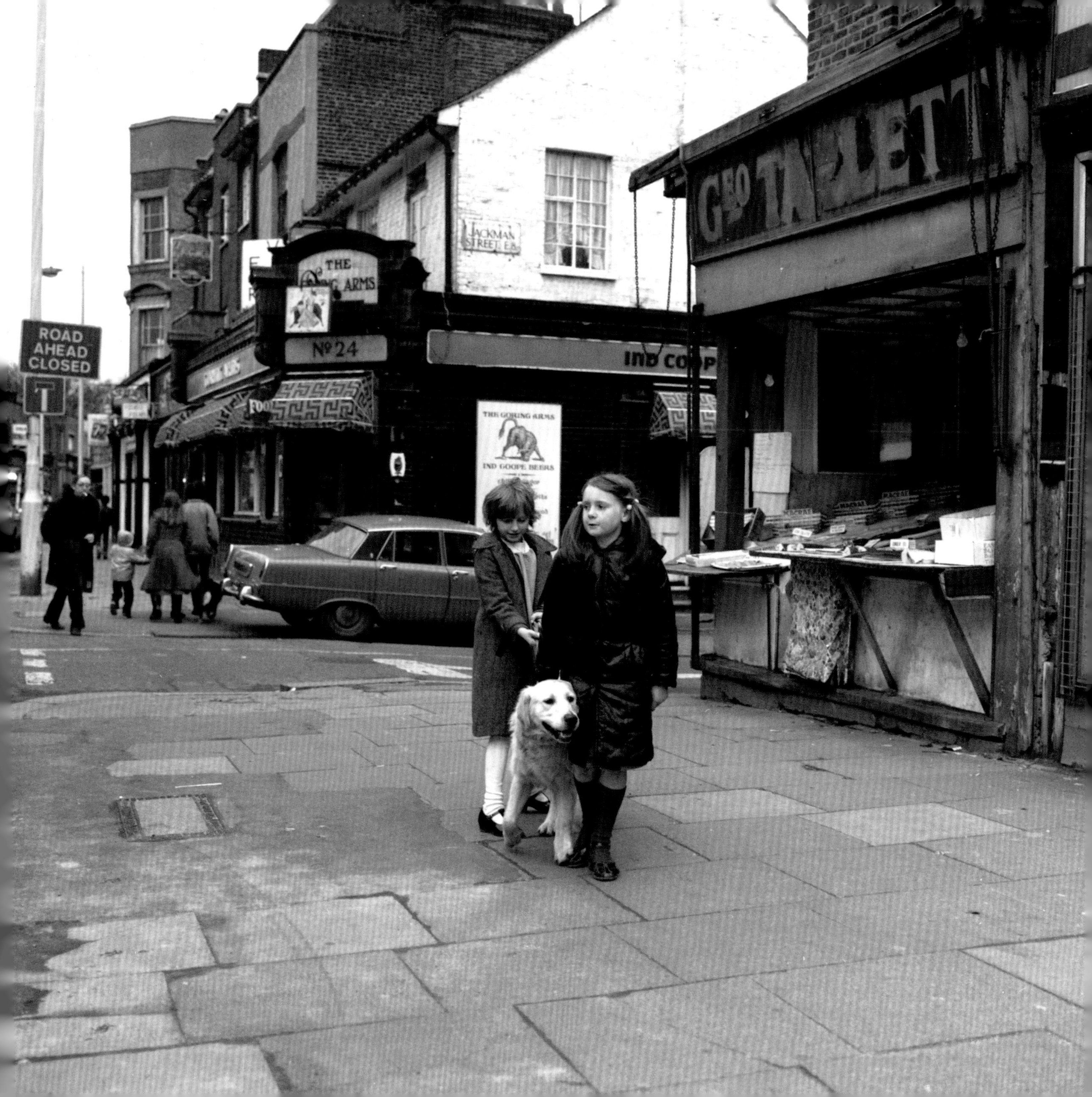
ROAD AHEAD CLOSED
JACKMAN STREET E8
№24
THE GORING ARMS
IND COOPE BEERS

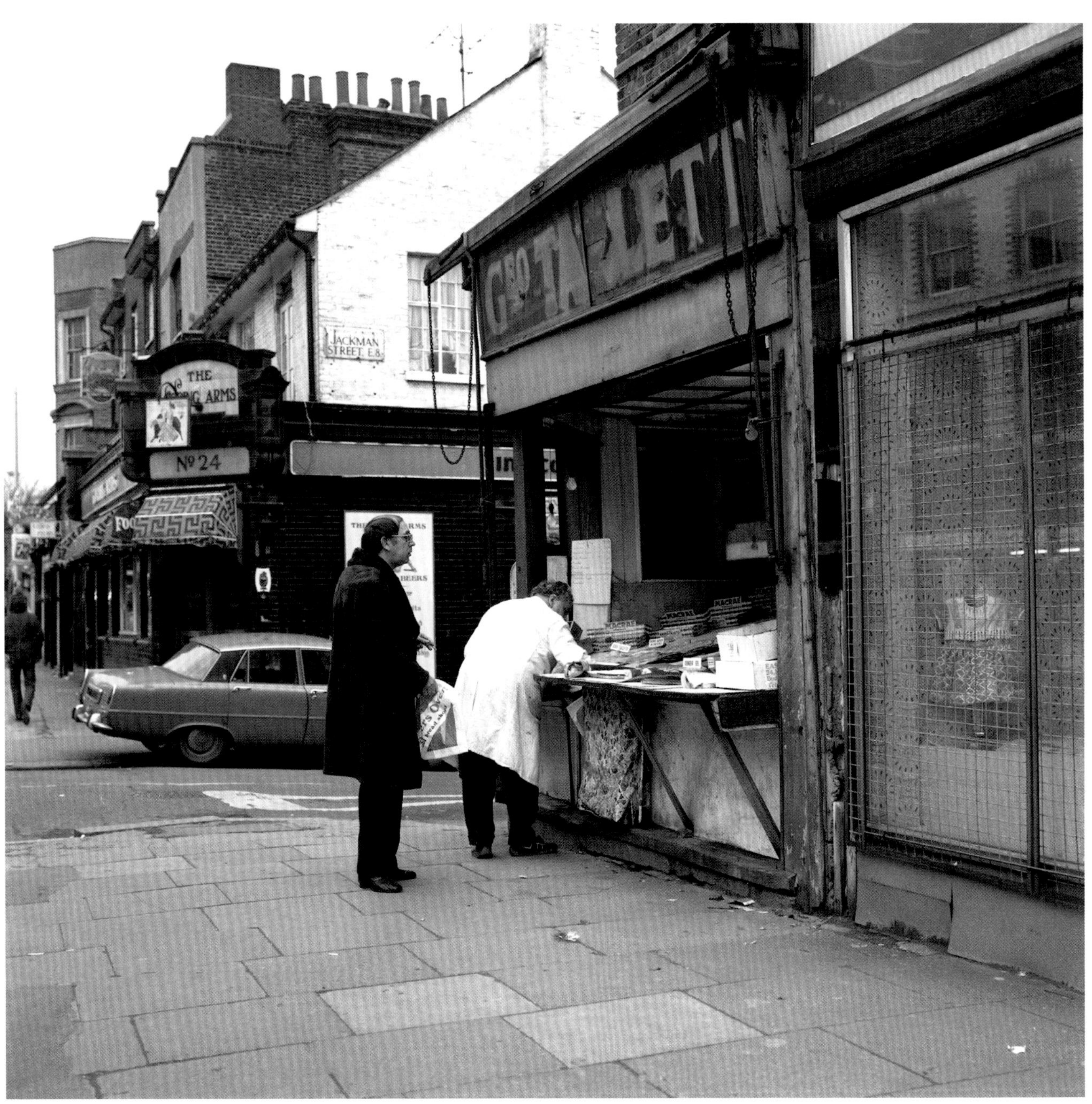

JACKMAN
STREET, E.8
THE
ARMS
Nº24

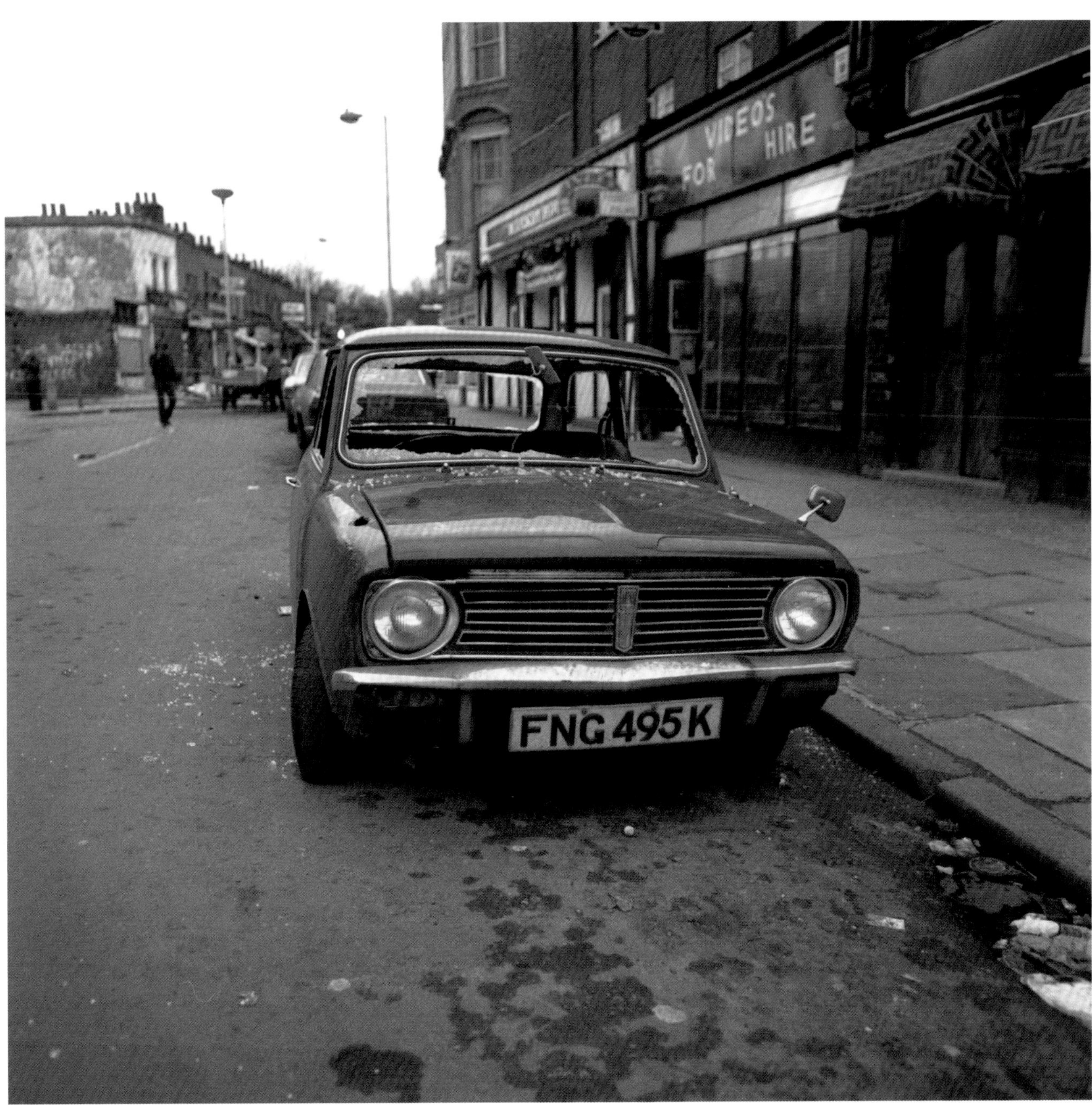
VIDEO'S
FOR HIRE
FNG 495 K

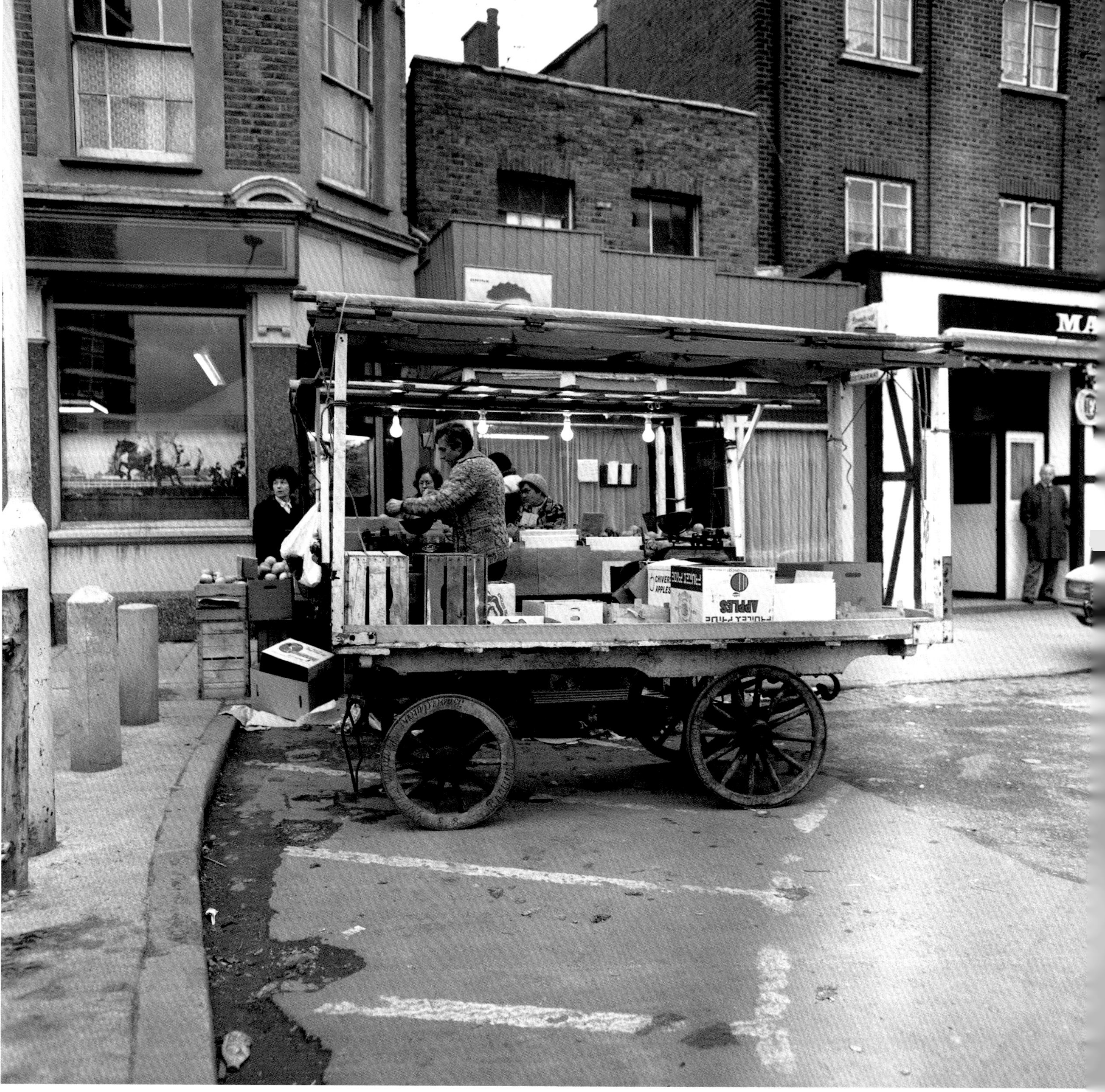
CHIVERS
APPLES

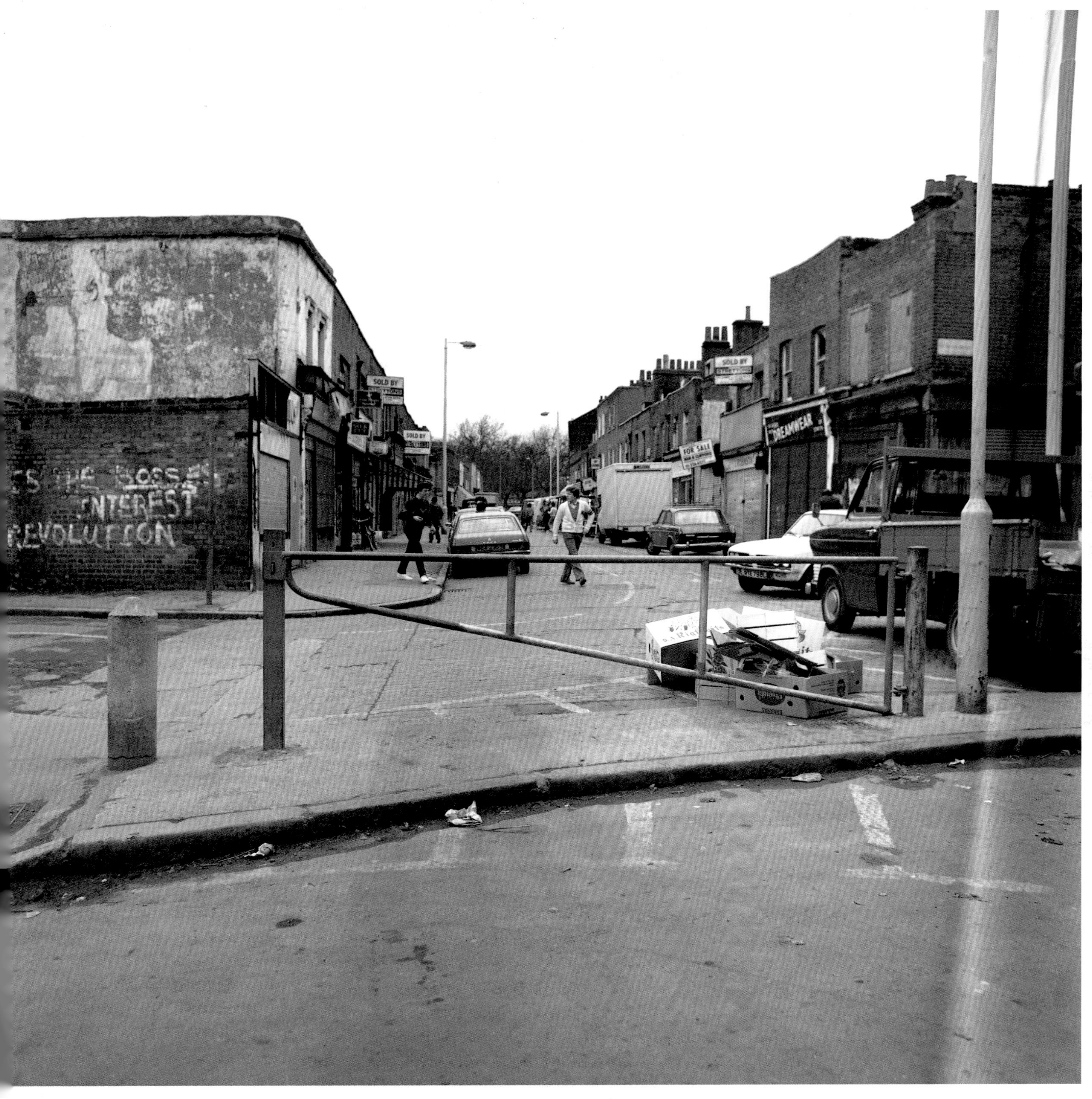
THE BOSS
INTEREST
REVOLUTION
SOLD BY
SOLD BY
FOR SALE
DREAMWEAR

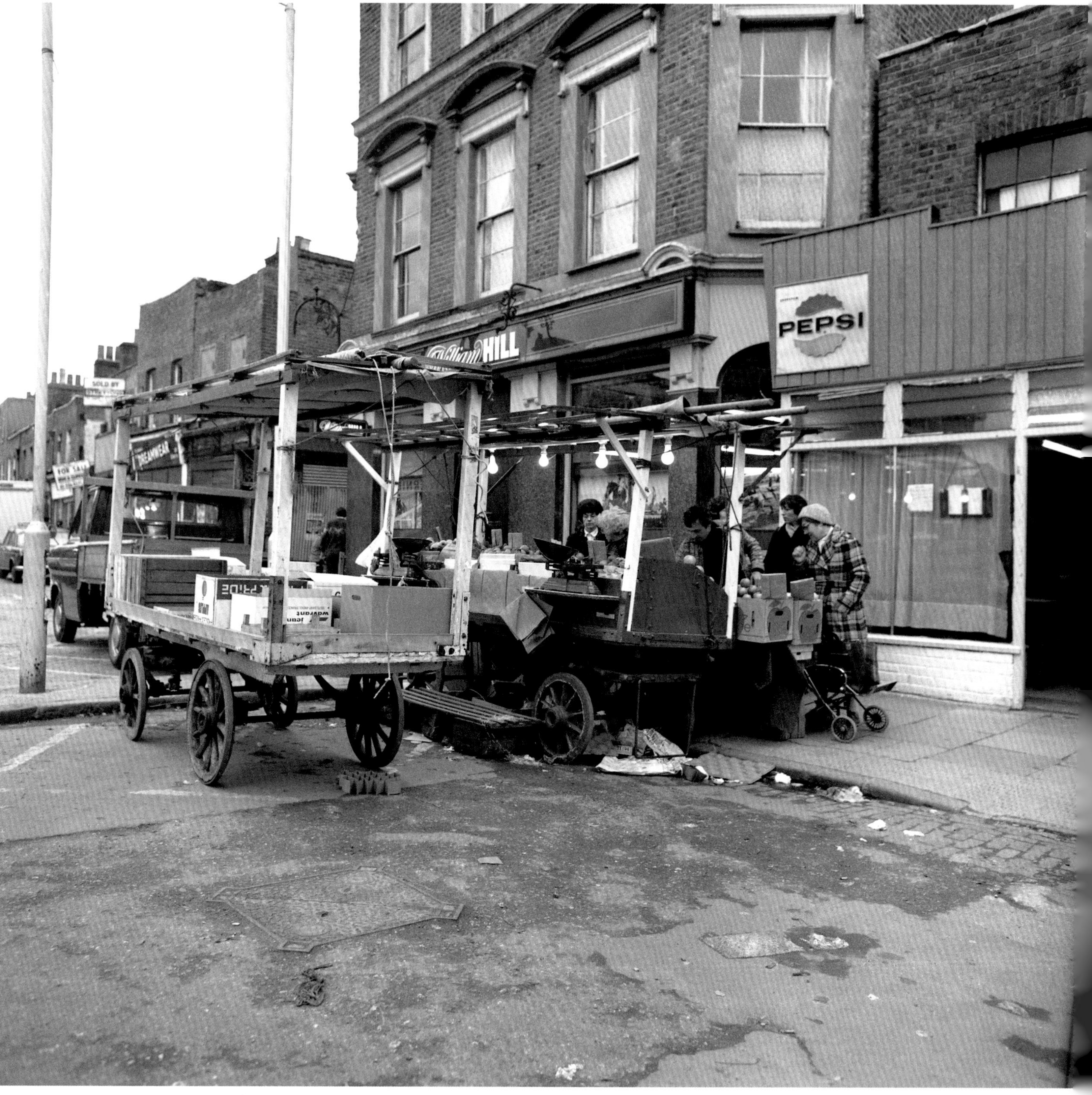
PEPSI
HILL
DREAMWEAR

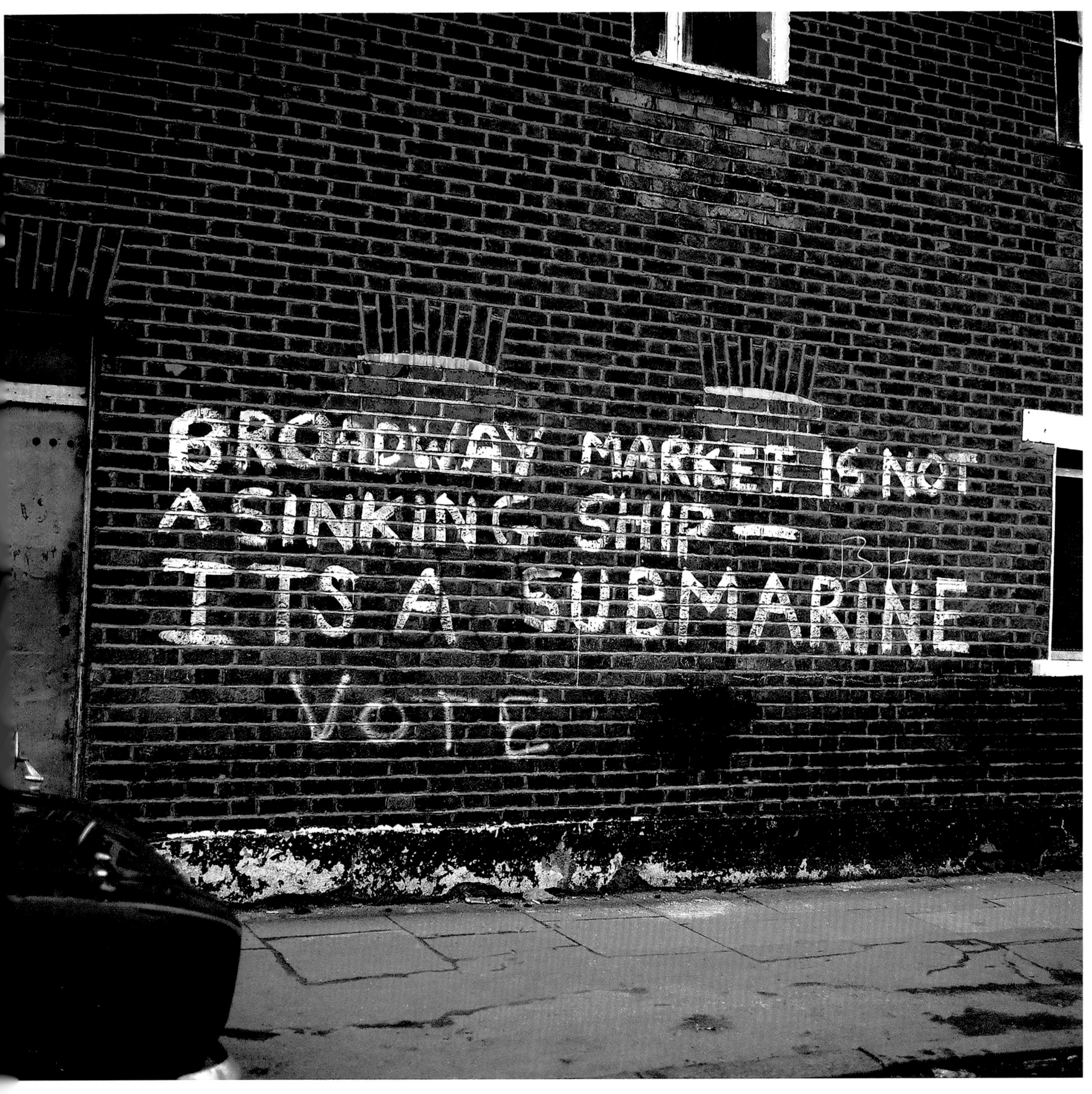
BROADWAY MARKET IS NOT
A SINKING SHIP –
ITS A SUBMARINE
VOTE

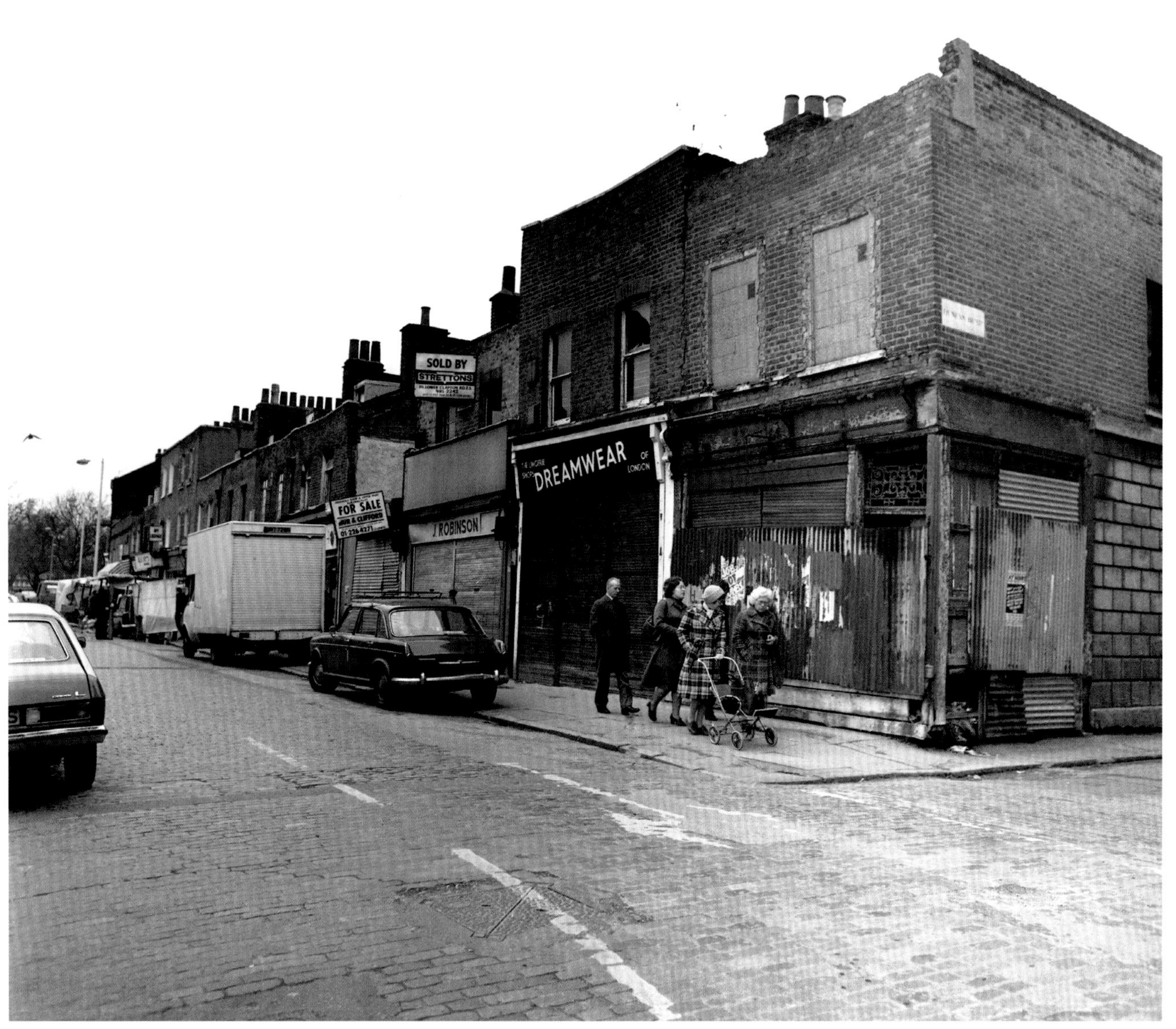
SOLD BY
STRETTONS
FOR SALE
01 226 4271
J. ROBINSON
THE LINGERIE SHOPS
DREAMWEAR
OF LONDON

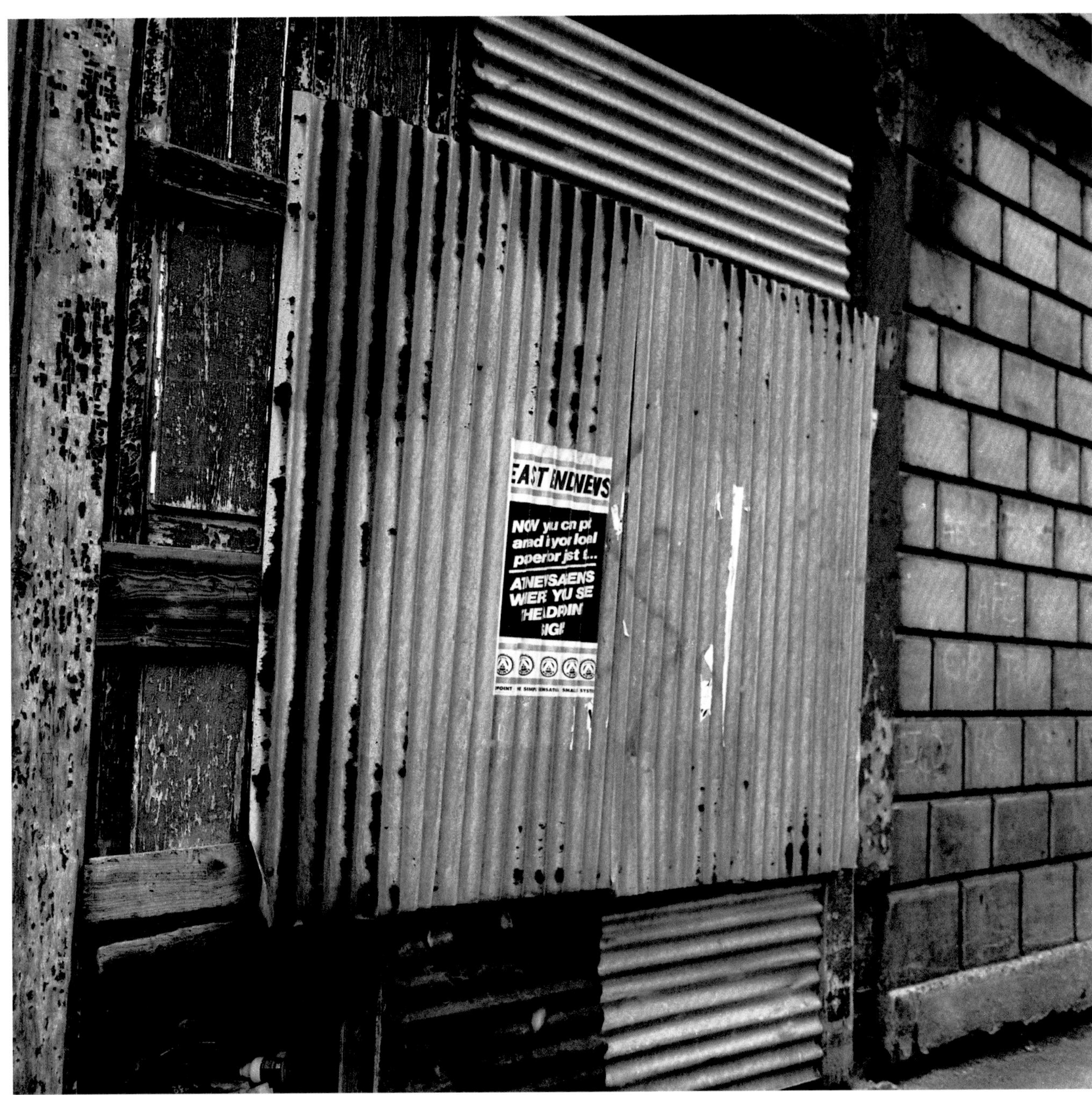
EAST ENDNEWS
NOW yu cn pt
arad i yor loal
pperor jst t...
ATNEVSAENS
WIER YU SE
THEADPIN
SIGI

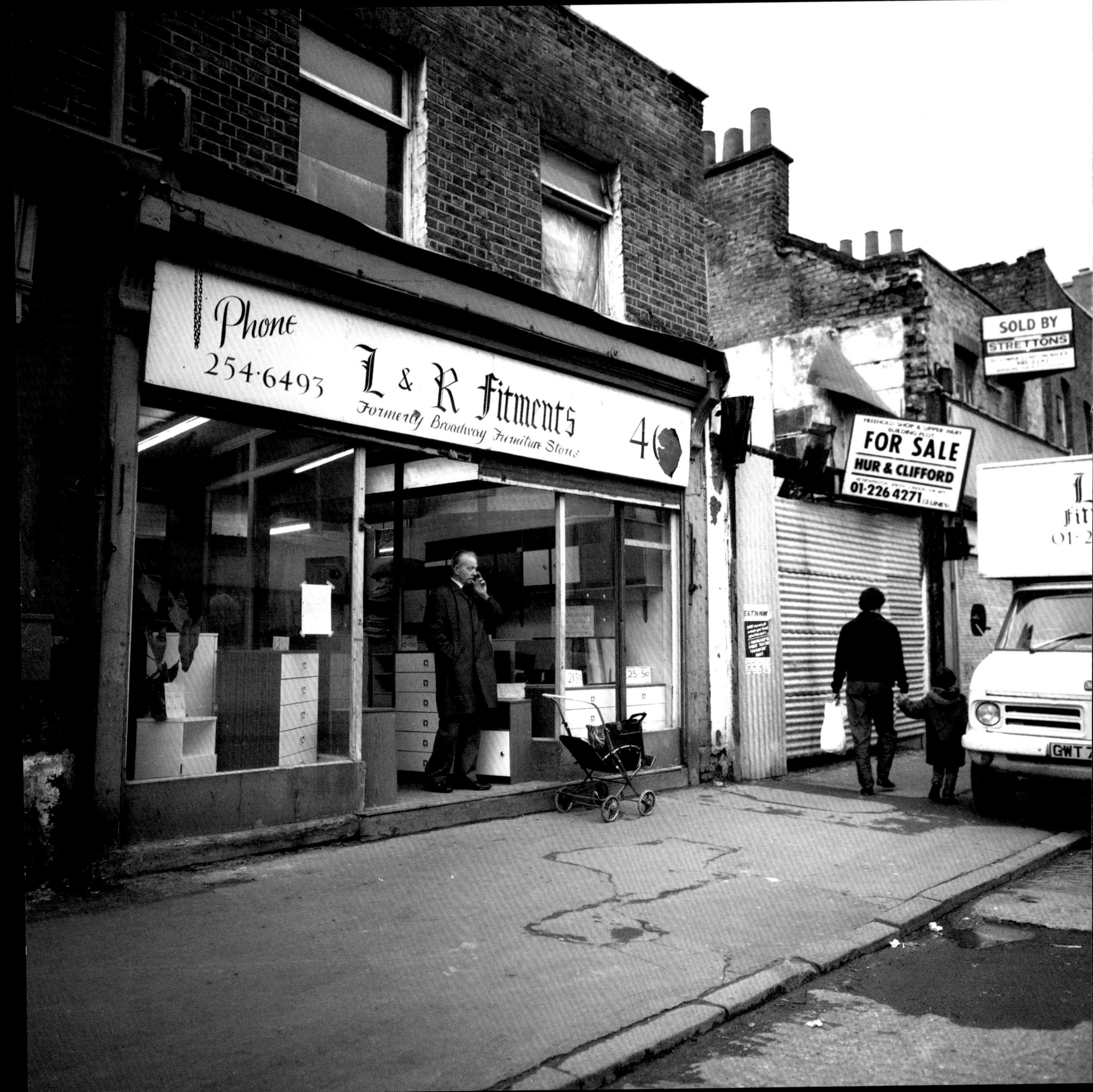

Phone
254·6493
L & R Fitments
Formerly Broadway Furniture Stores
SOLD BY
STRETTONS
FOR SALE
HUR & CLIFFORD
01·226 4271

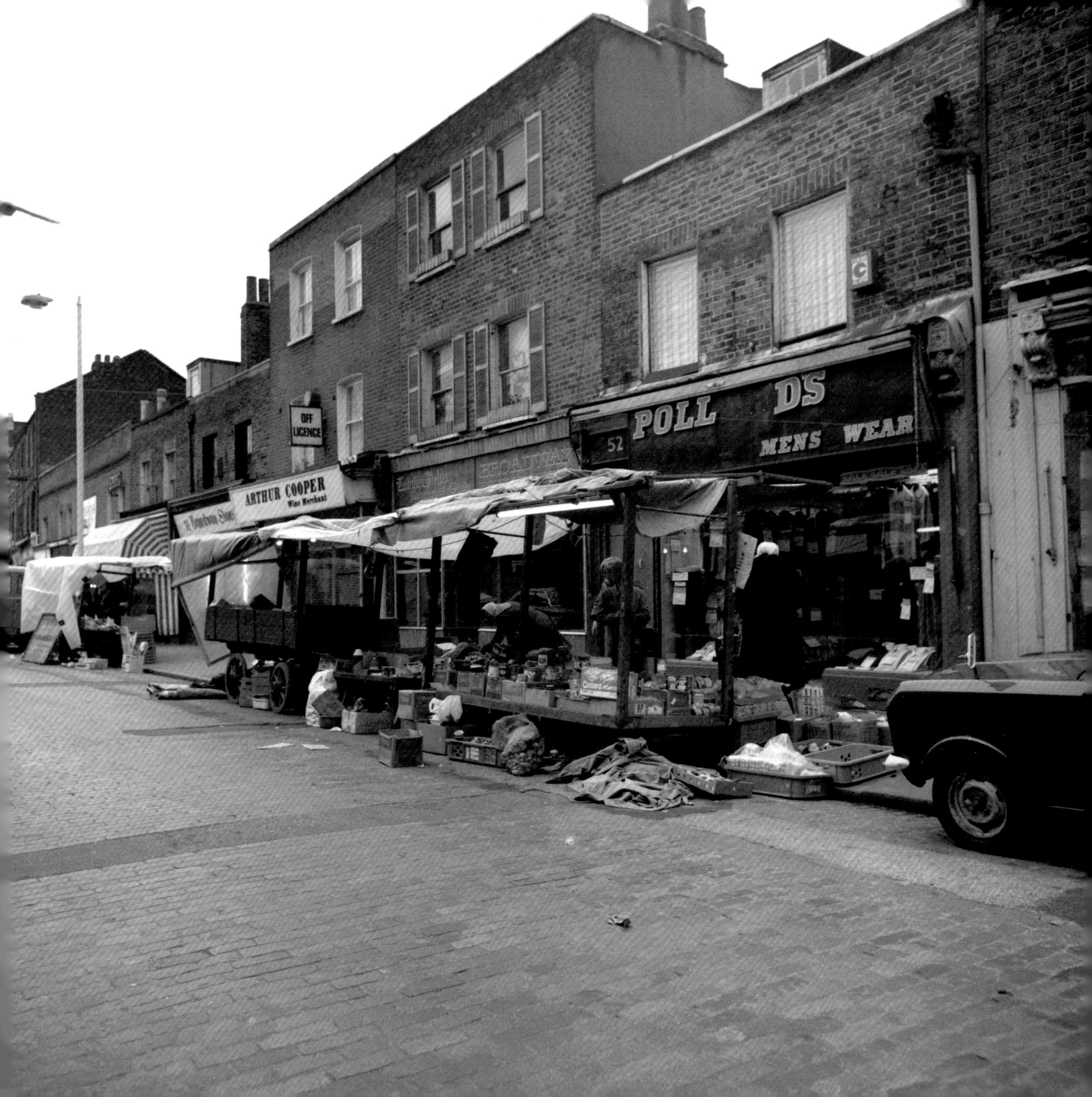

OFF LICENCE
ARTHUR COOPER
Wine Merchant
52
POLL
DS
MENS
WEAR

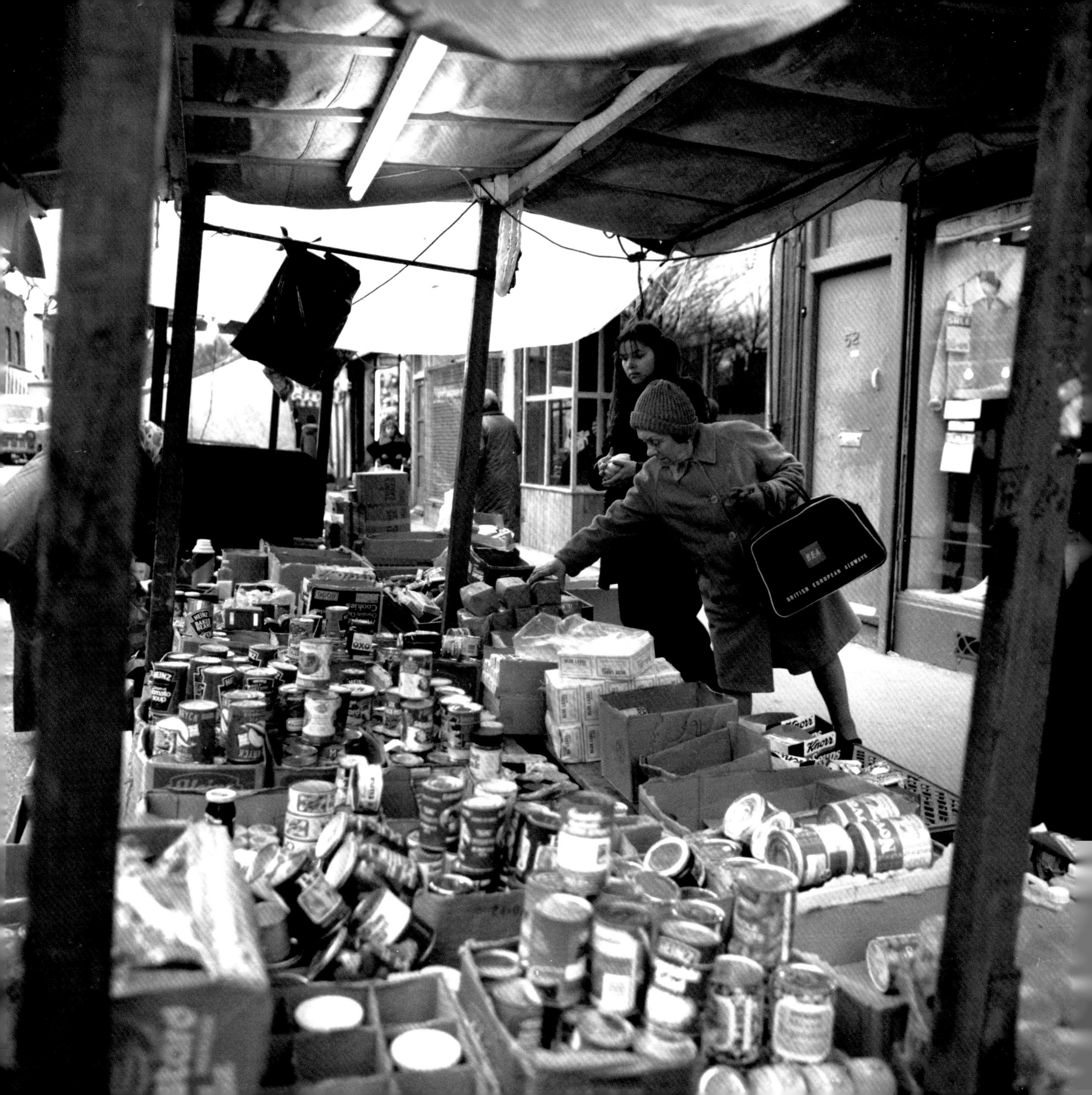

BEA
BRITISH EUROPEAN AIRWAYS
52
HEINZ
Tomato soup
OXO
Cookies
Knorr

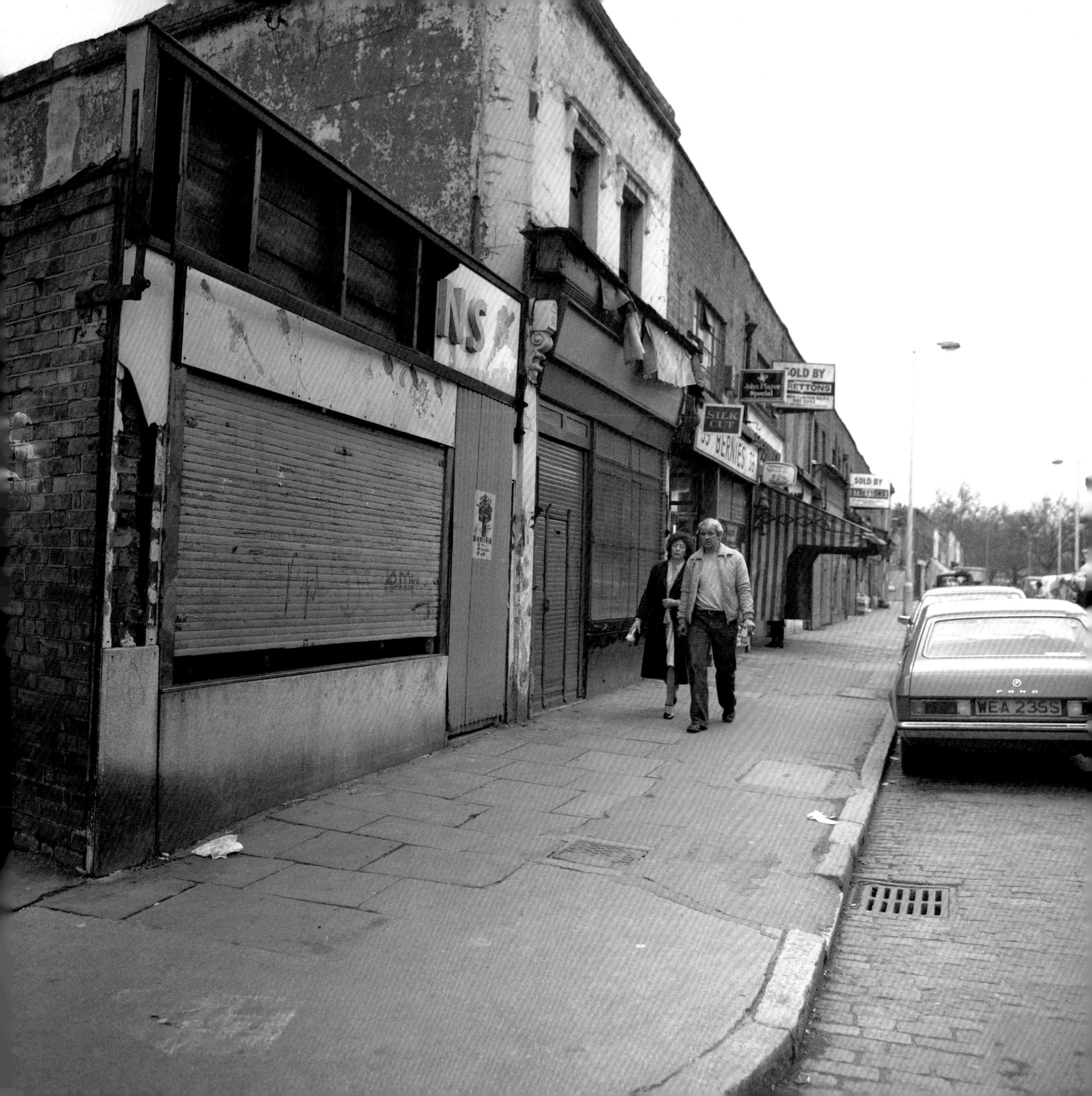

NS
SOLD BY
RETTONS
John Player Special
SILK CUT
BERNIES 35
SOLD BY
FORD
WEA 235S

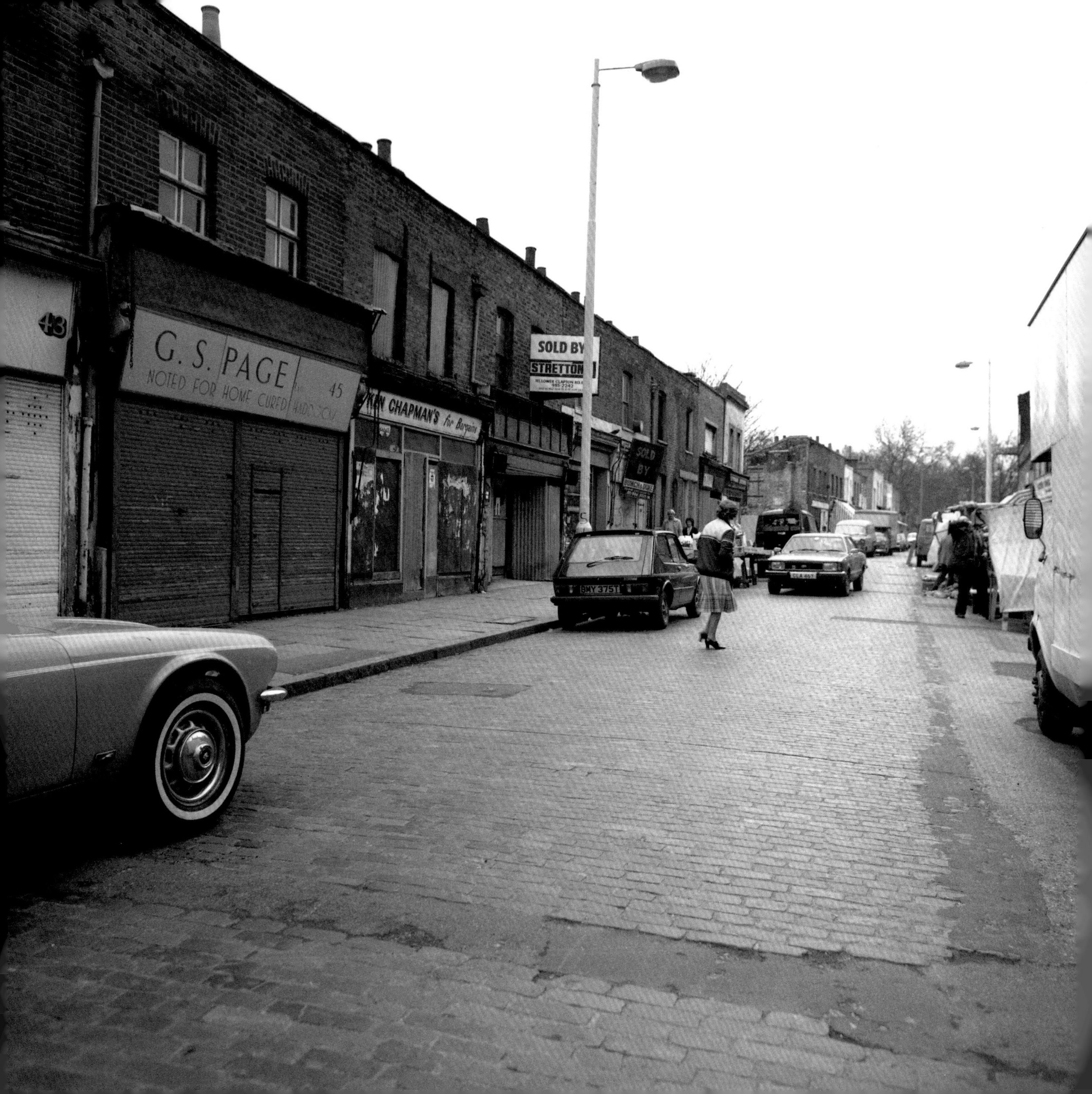
43
G. S. PAGE
NOTED FOR HOME CURED
45
CHAPMAN'S
SOLD BY
STRETTON
SOLD
BY
BMY 375T

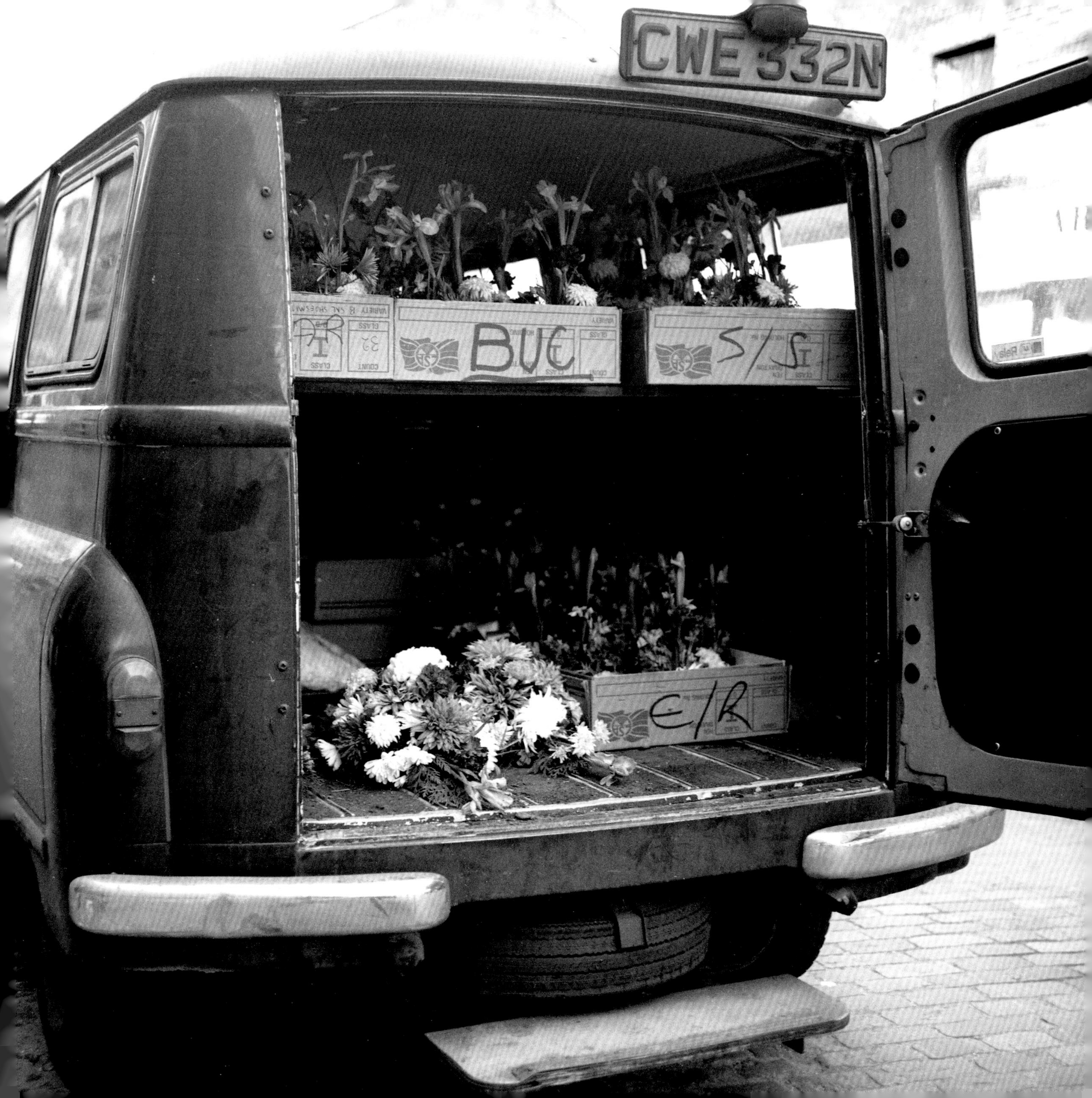
CWE 332N
BUC
E/R

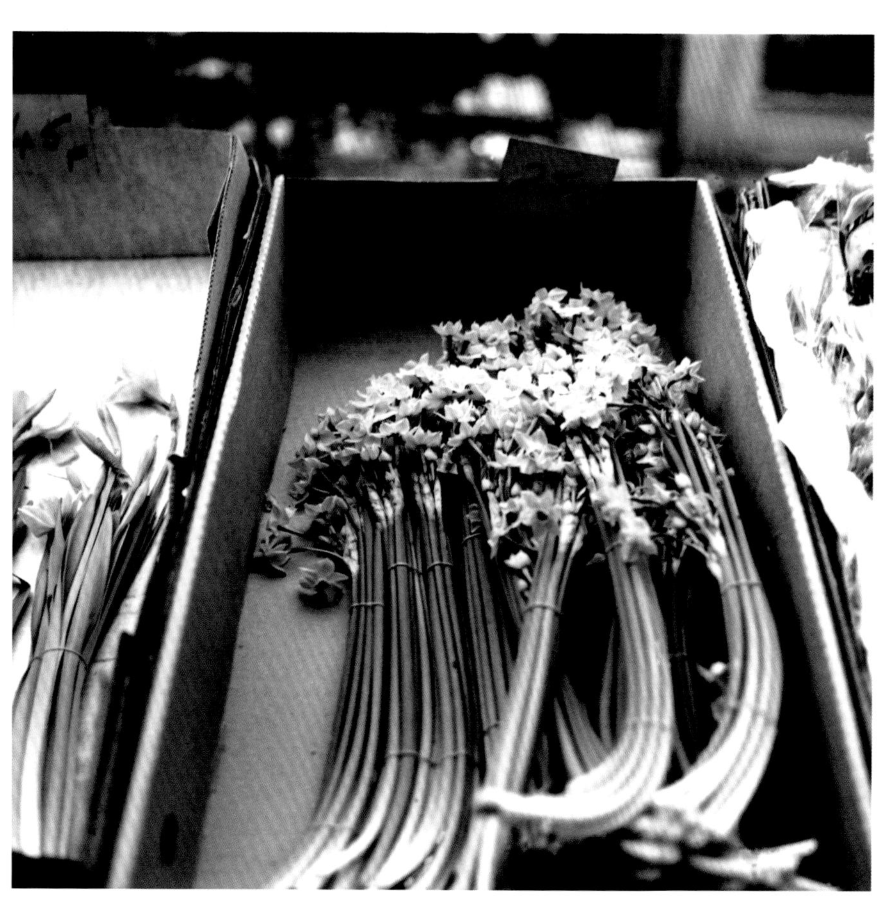

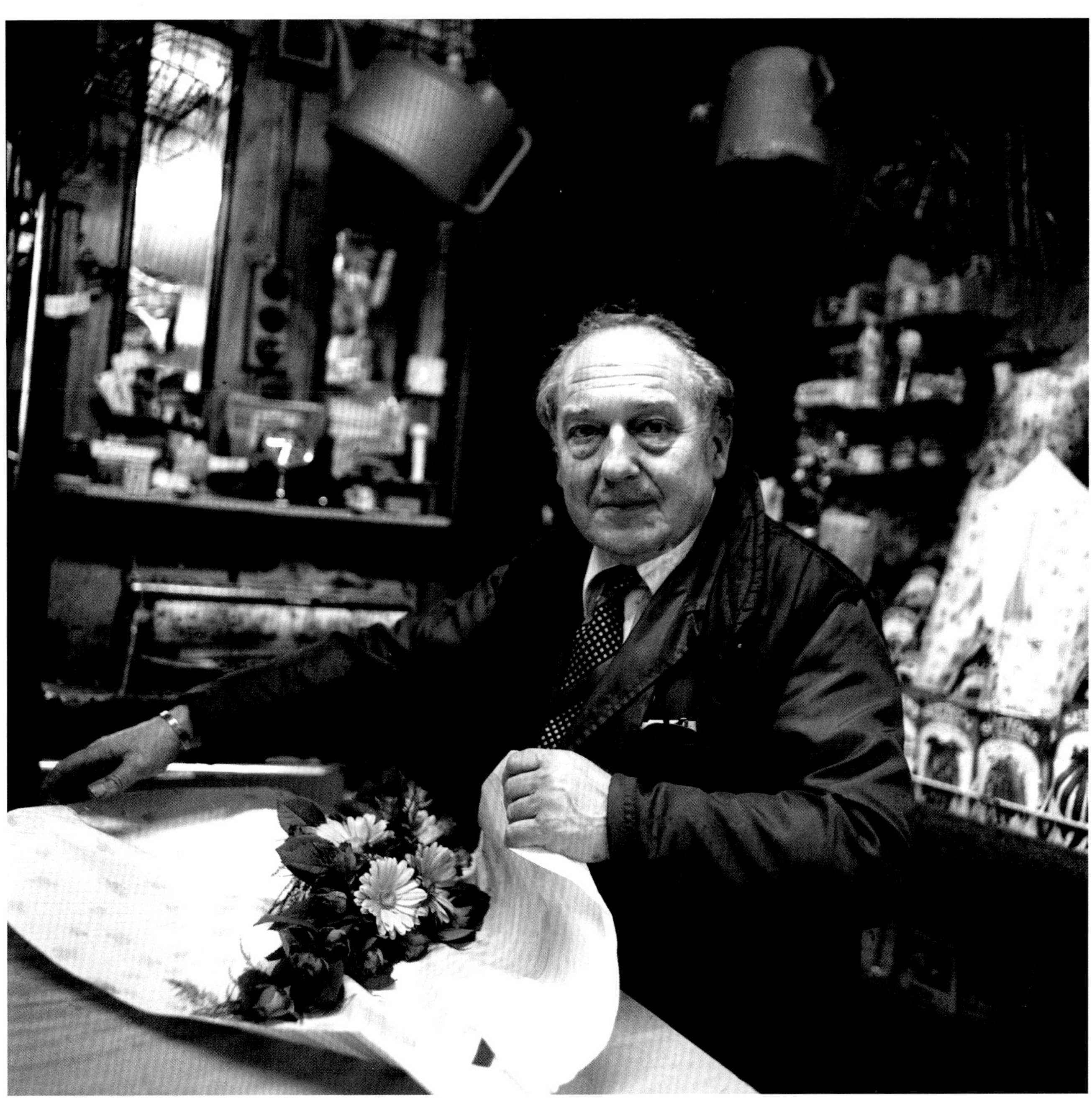

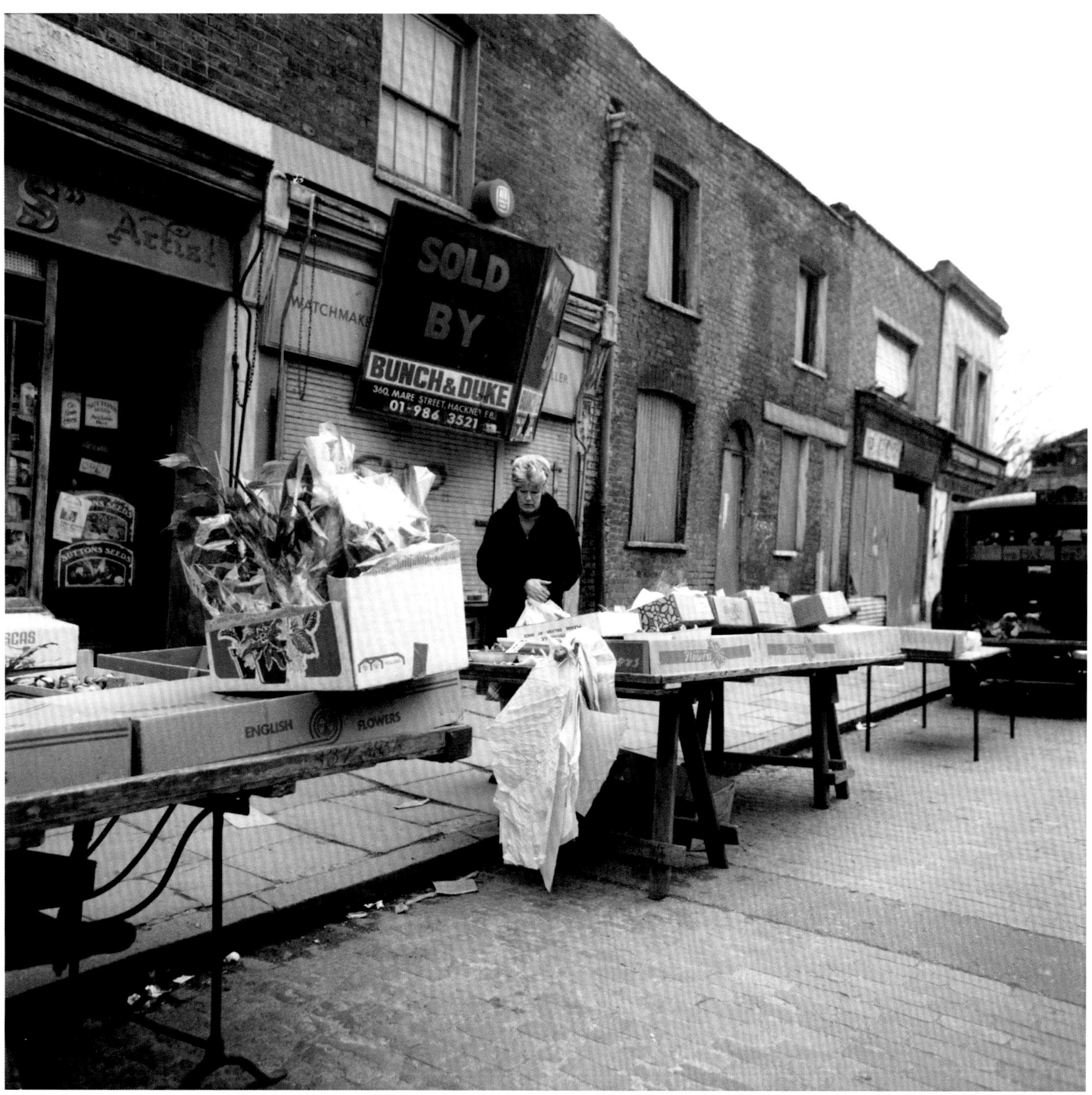
SOLD BY
BUNCH & DUKE
360, MARE STREET, HACKNEY
01-986 3521
WATCHMAKE
SUTTONS SEEDS
SUTTONS SEEDS
ENGLISH FLOWERS

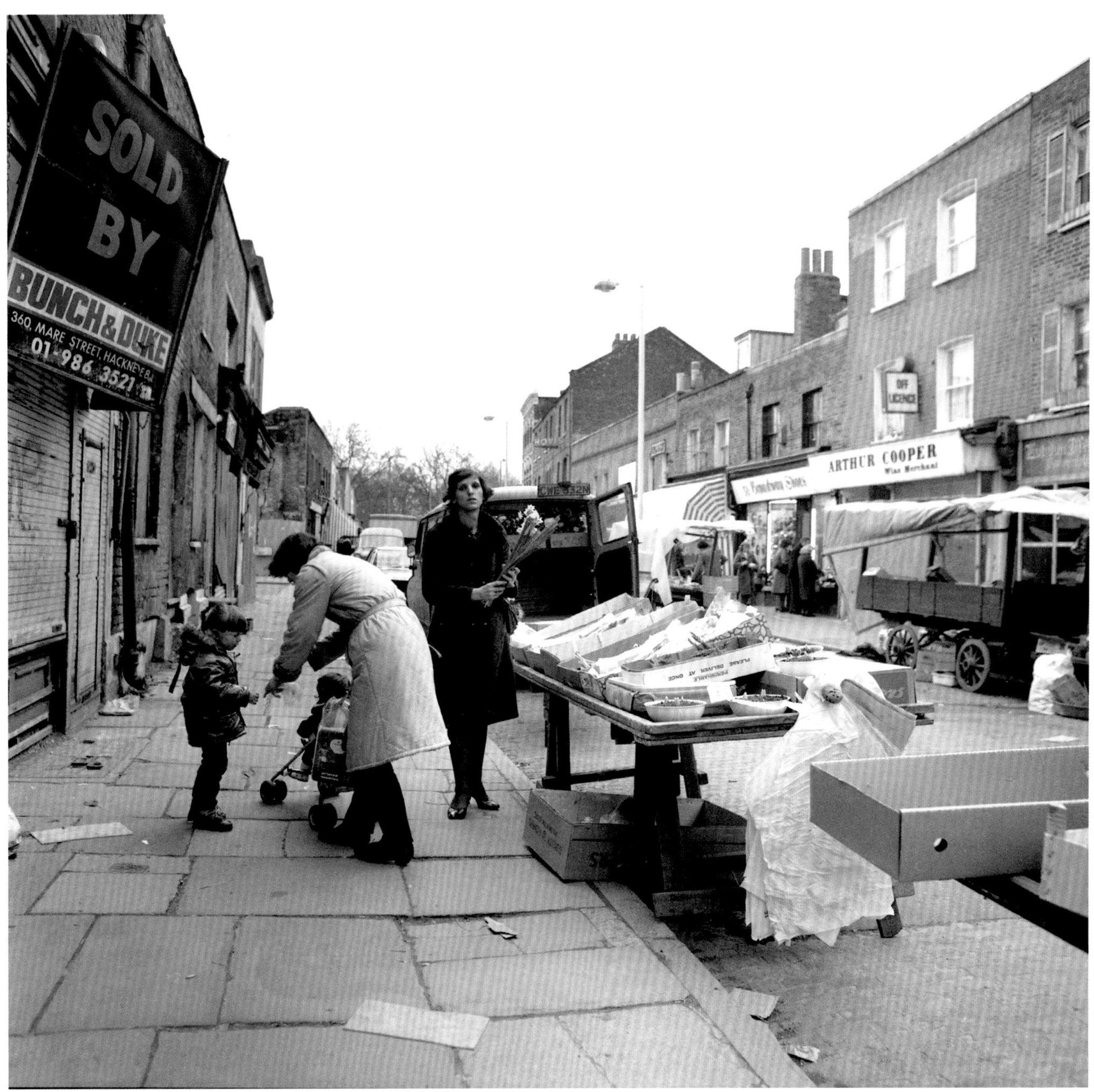
SOLD
BY
BUNCH&DUKE
360, MARE STREET, HACKNEY
01·986 3521
OFF
LICENCE
ARTHUR COOPER
Wine Merchant

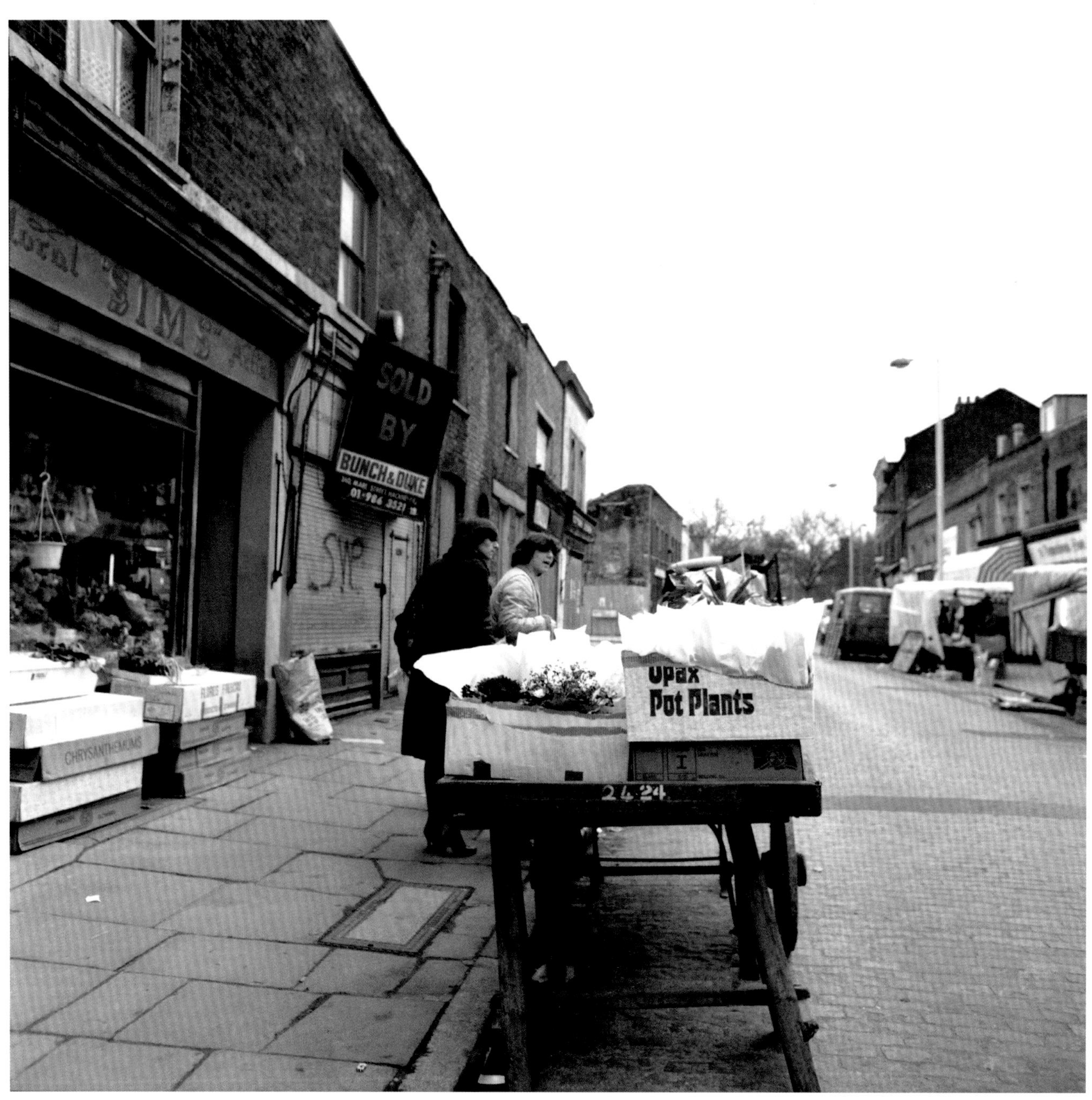
SIMS
SOLD BY
BUNCH & DUKE
CHRYSANTHEMUMS
Pot Plants
2424

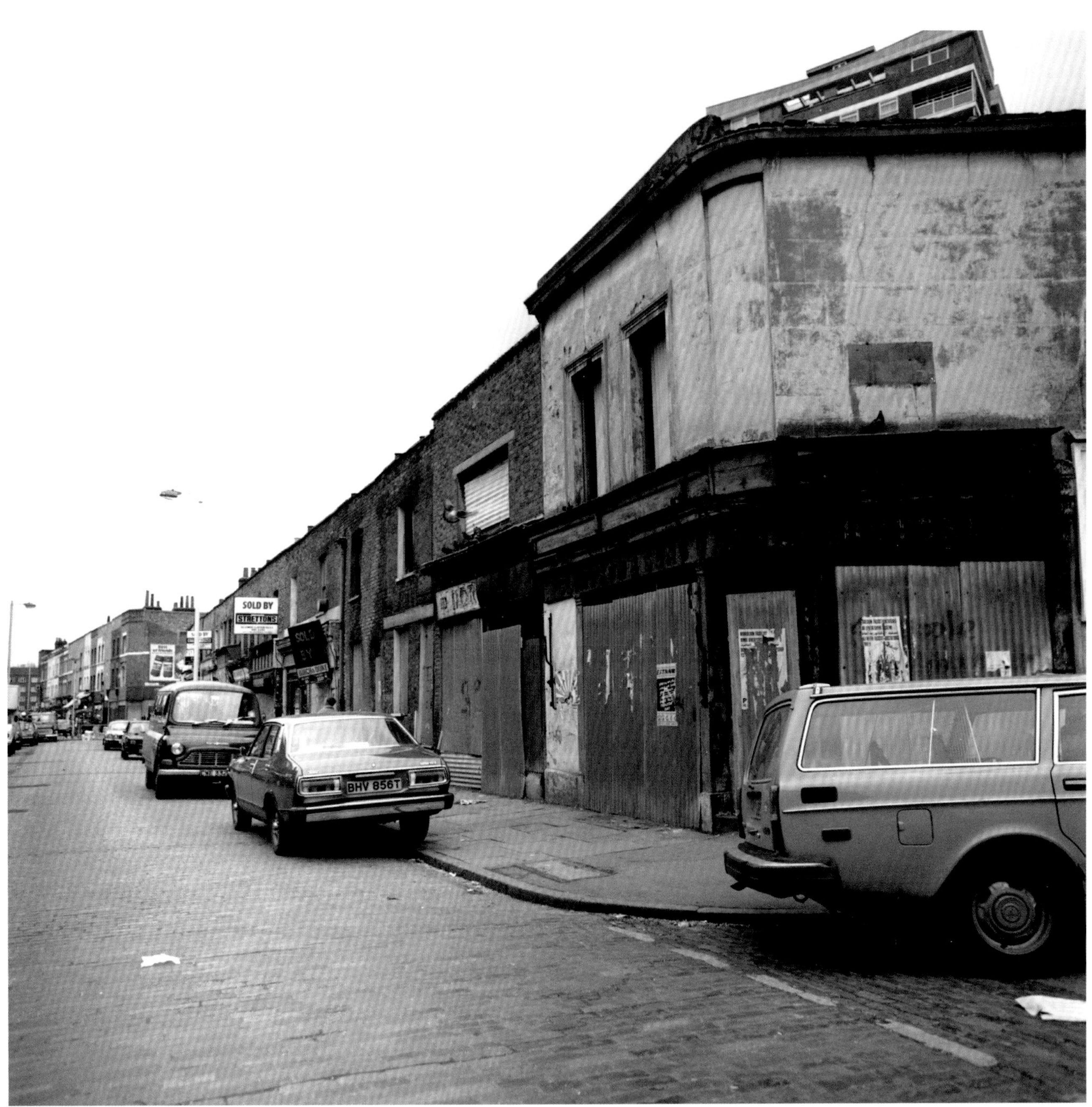
SOLD BY
STRETTONS
BHV 856T

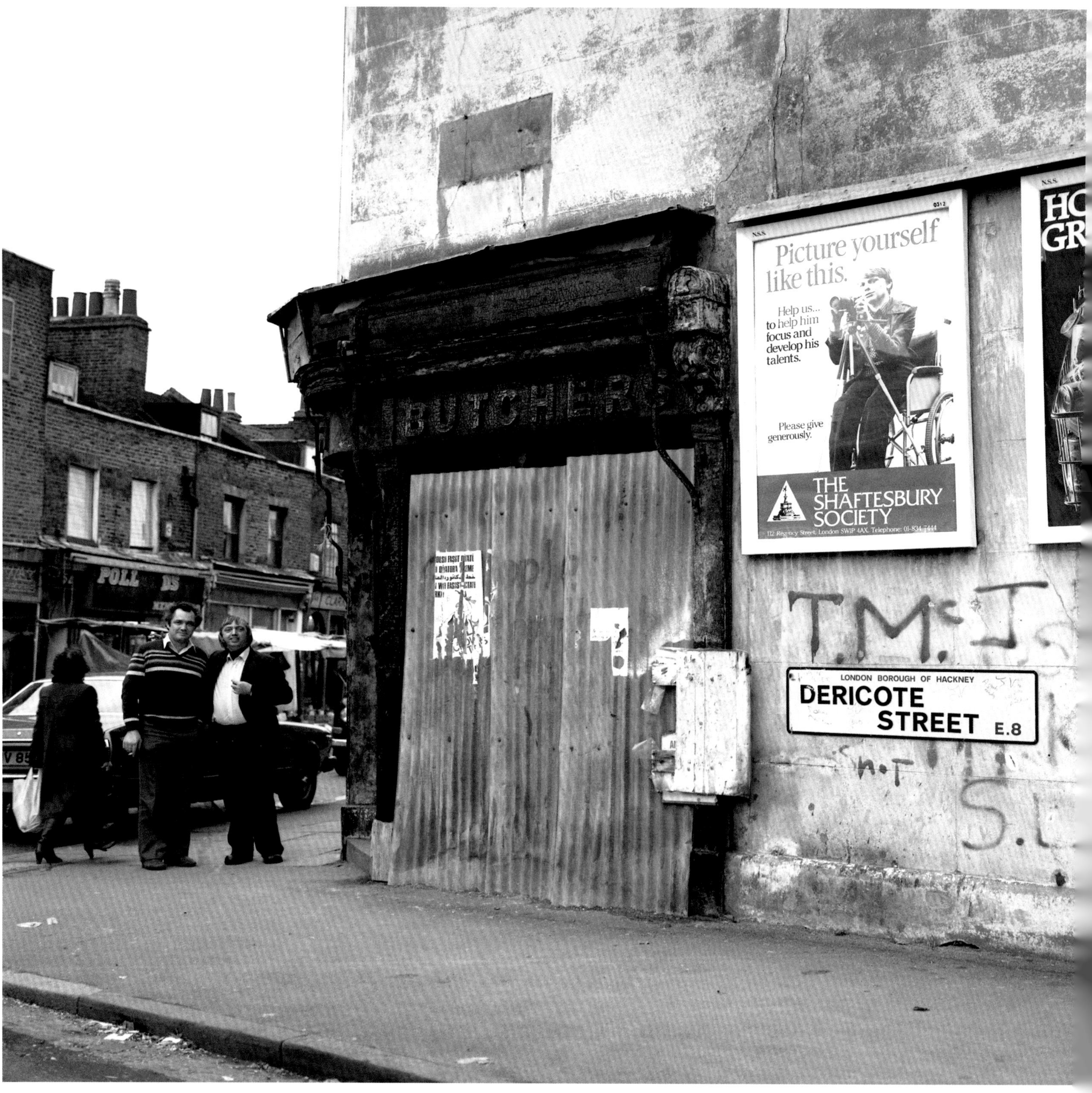
BUTCHER
Picture yourself like this.
Help us... to help him focus and develop his talents.
Please give generously.
THE SHAFTESBURY SOCIETY
LONDON BOROUGH OF HACKNEY
DERICOTE STREET E.8

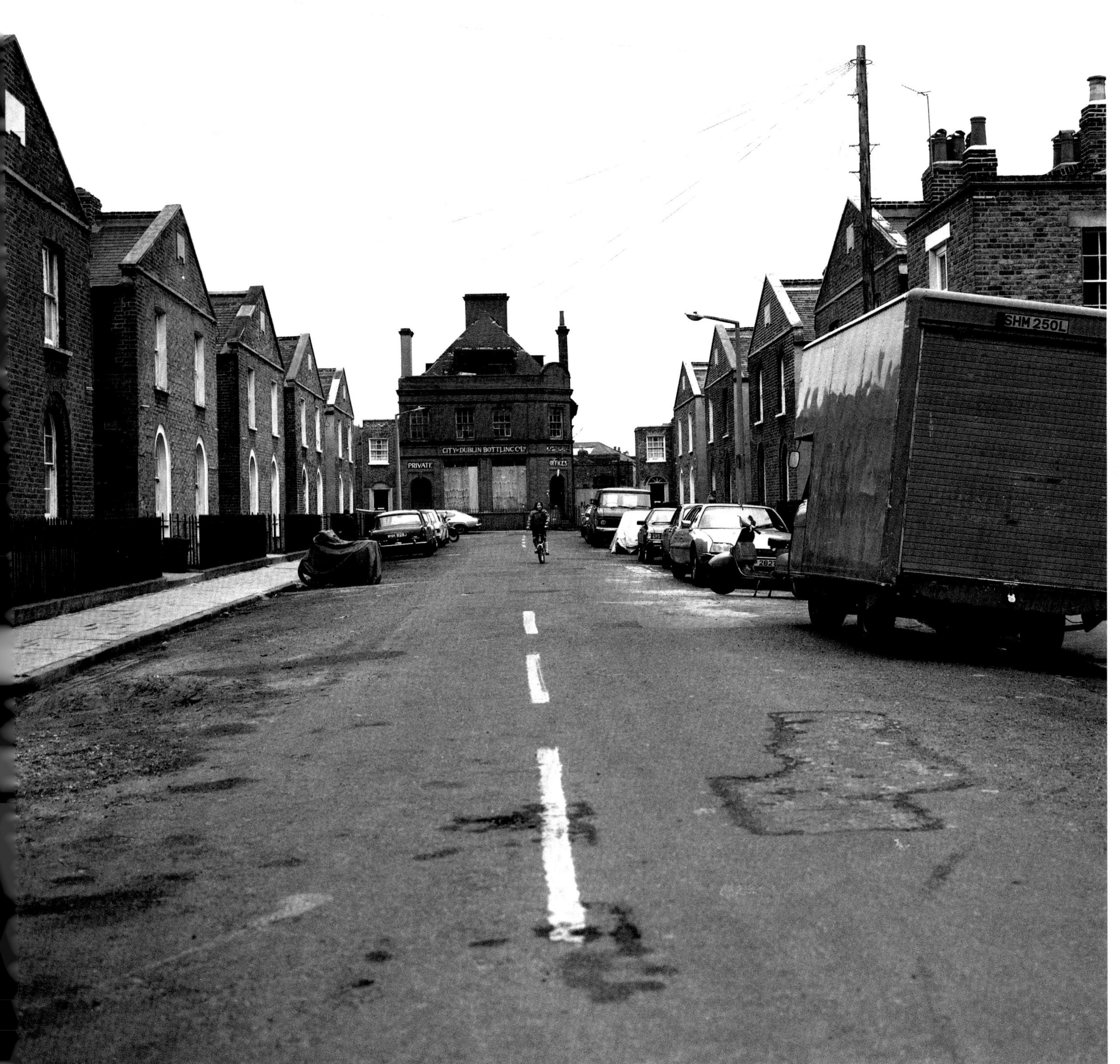
CITY of DUBLIN BOTTLING Co Ld
PRIVATE
OFFICES
SHM 250L

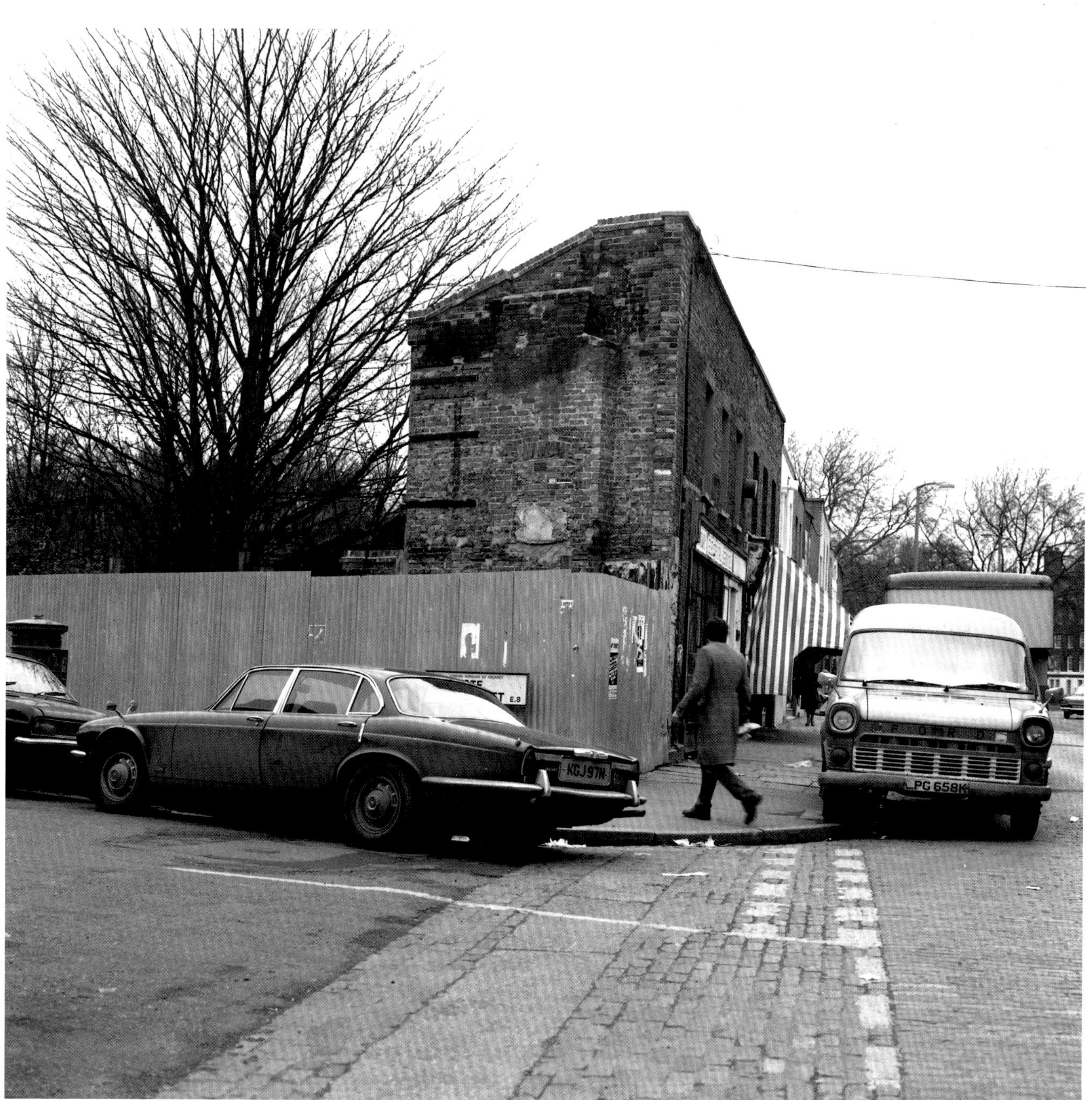
KGJ 97N
FORD
PG 658K

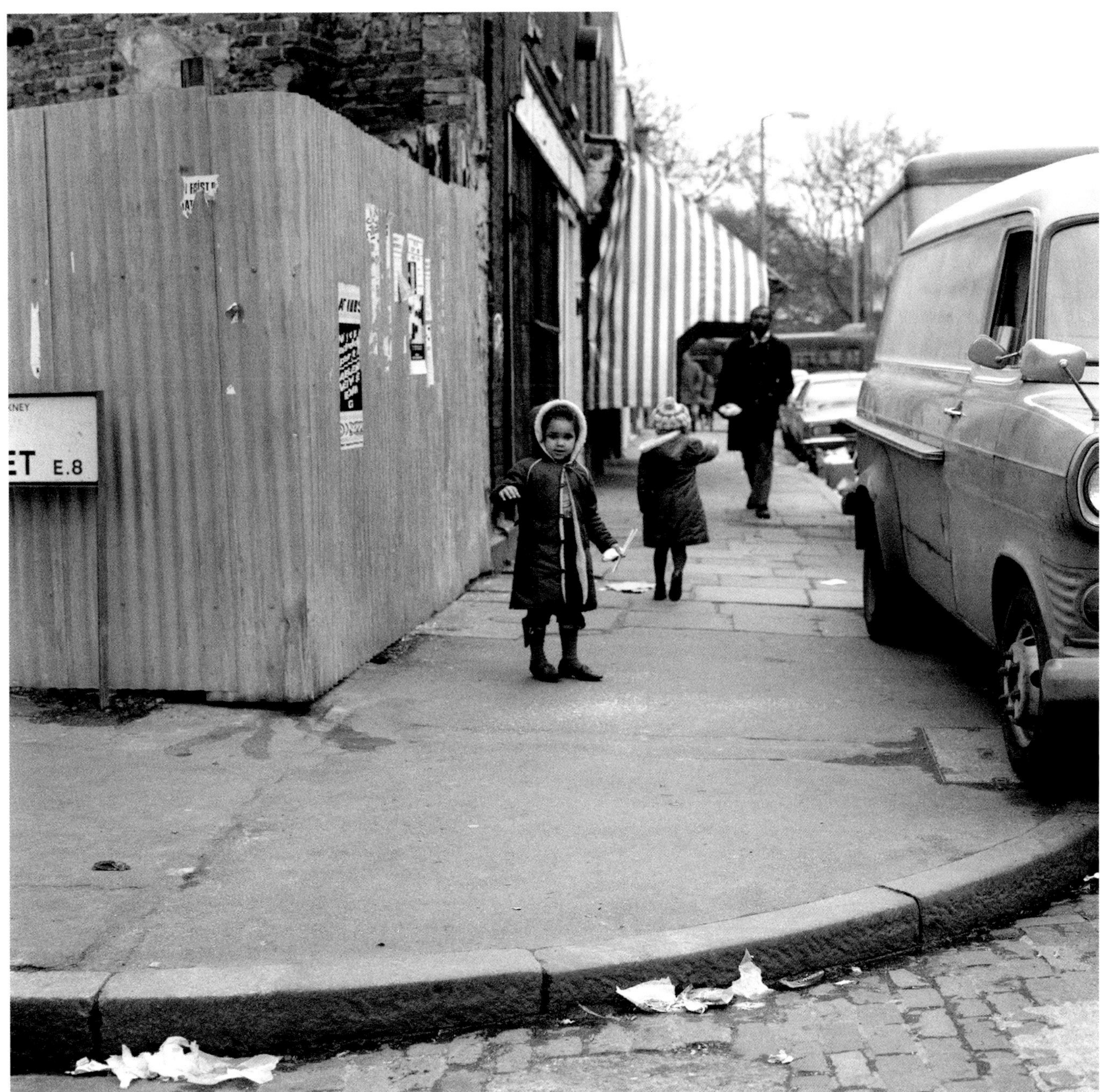
KNEY
ET E.8

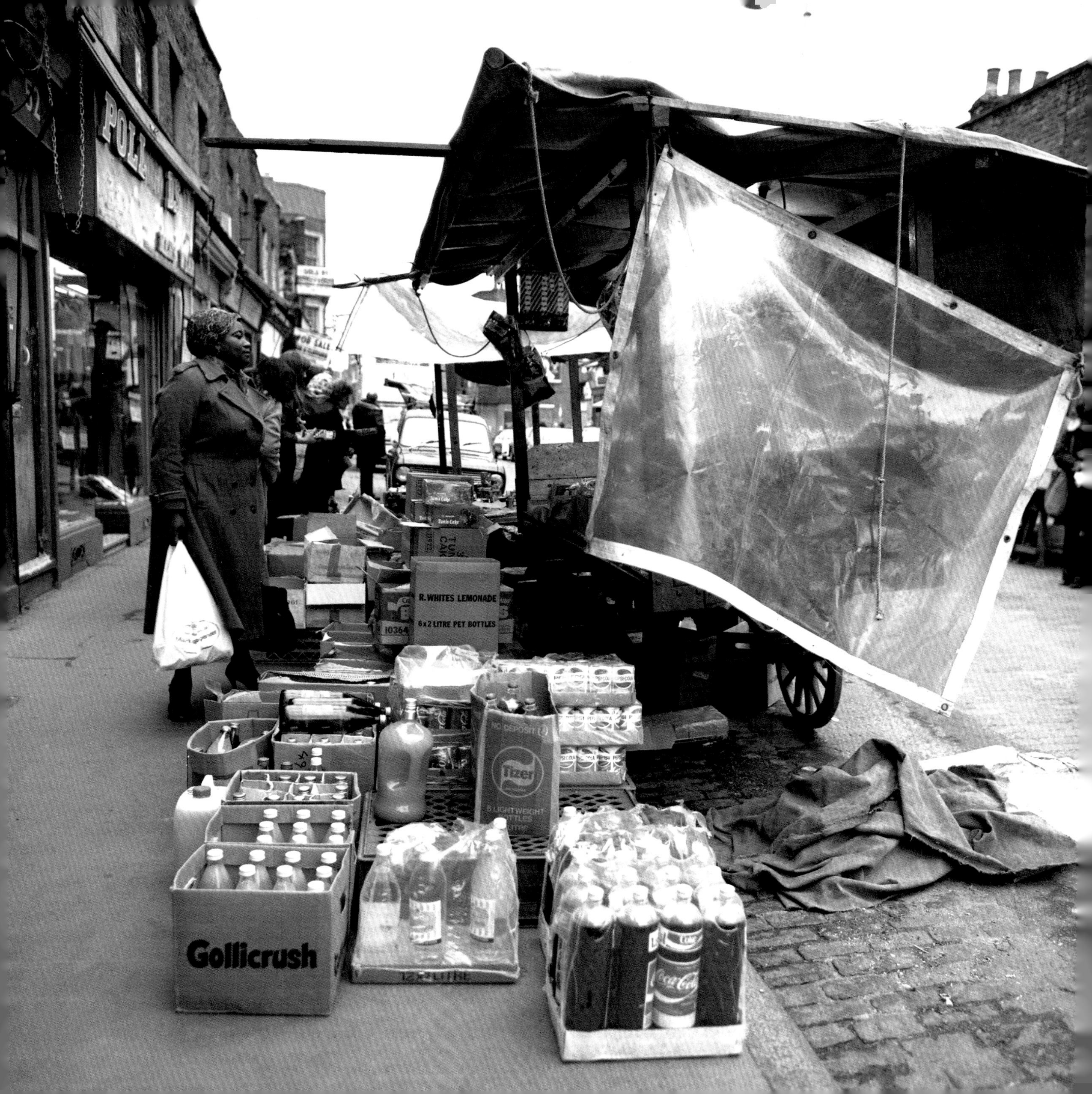
R. WHITES LEMONADE
6 x 2 LITRE PET BOTTLES
NO DEPOSIT
Tizer
6 LIGHTWEIGHT BOTTLES
Gollicrush
Coca-Cola

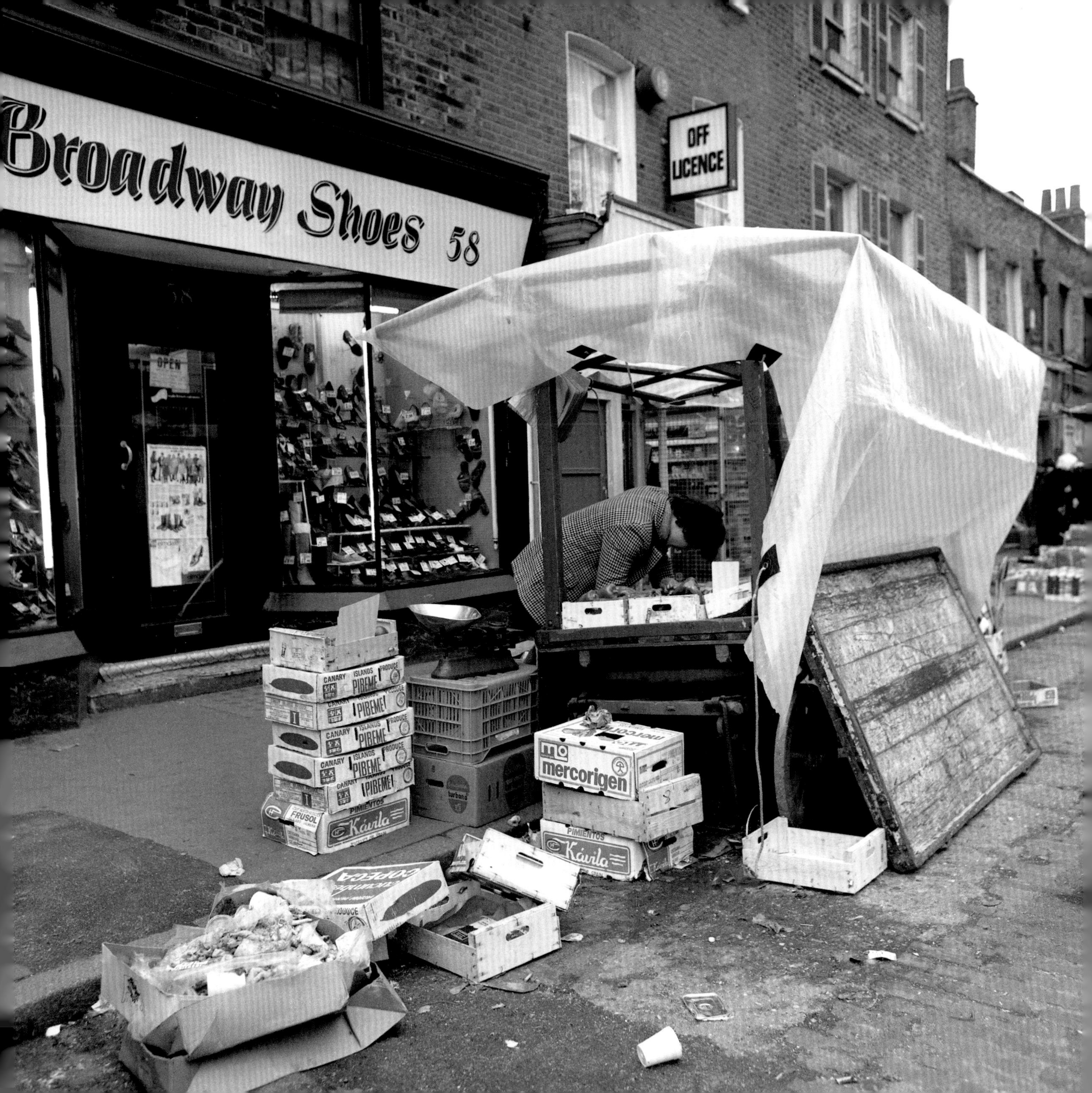
Broadway Shoes 58
OFF LICENCE
OPEN
CANARY ISLANDS PRODUCE
PIBEME
FRUSOL
PIMIENTOS
Kávila
mo
mercorigen

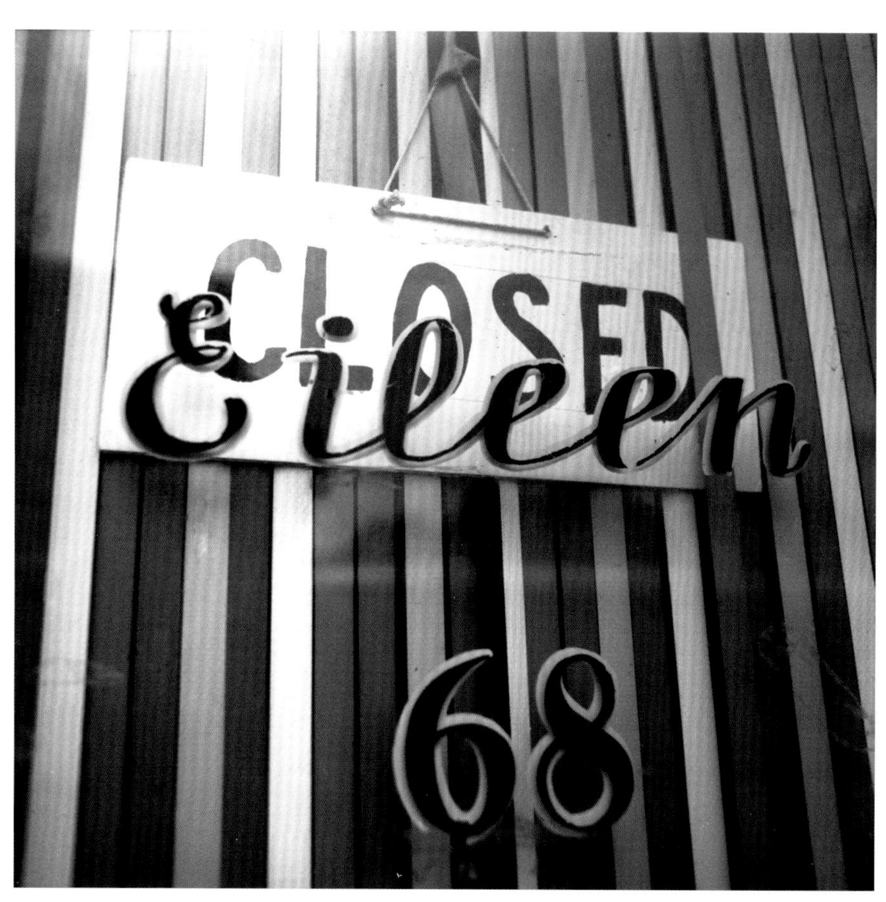
CLOSED
Eileen
68

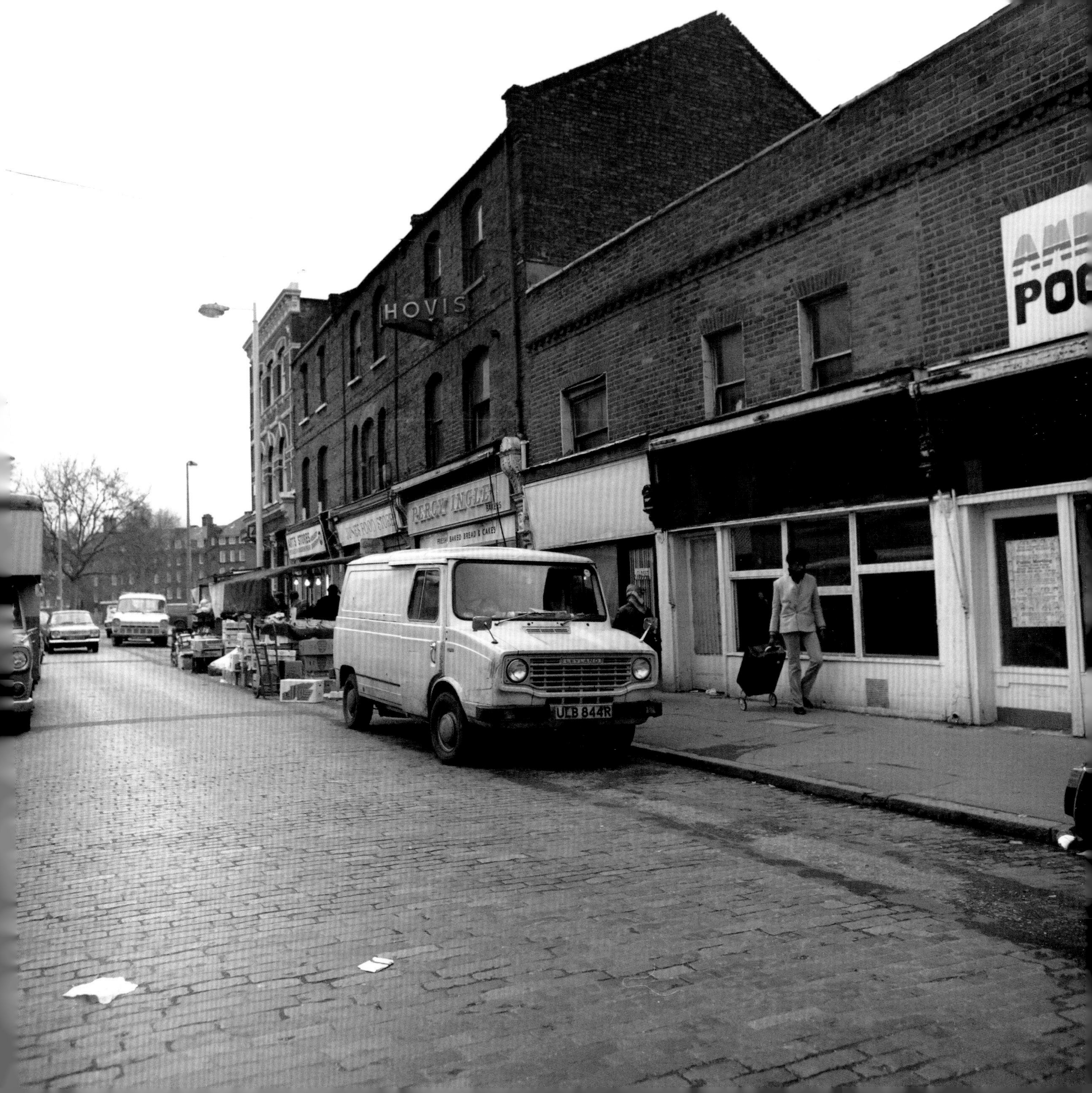
HOVIS
PERCY INGLE
BAKERS
FRESH BAKED BREAD & CAKES
LEYLAND
ULB 844R

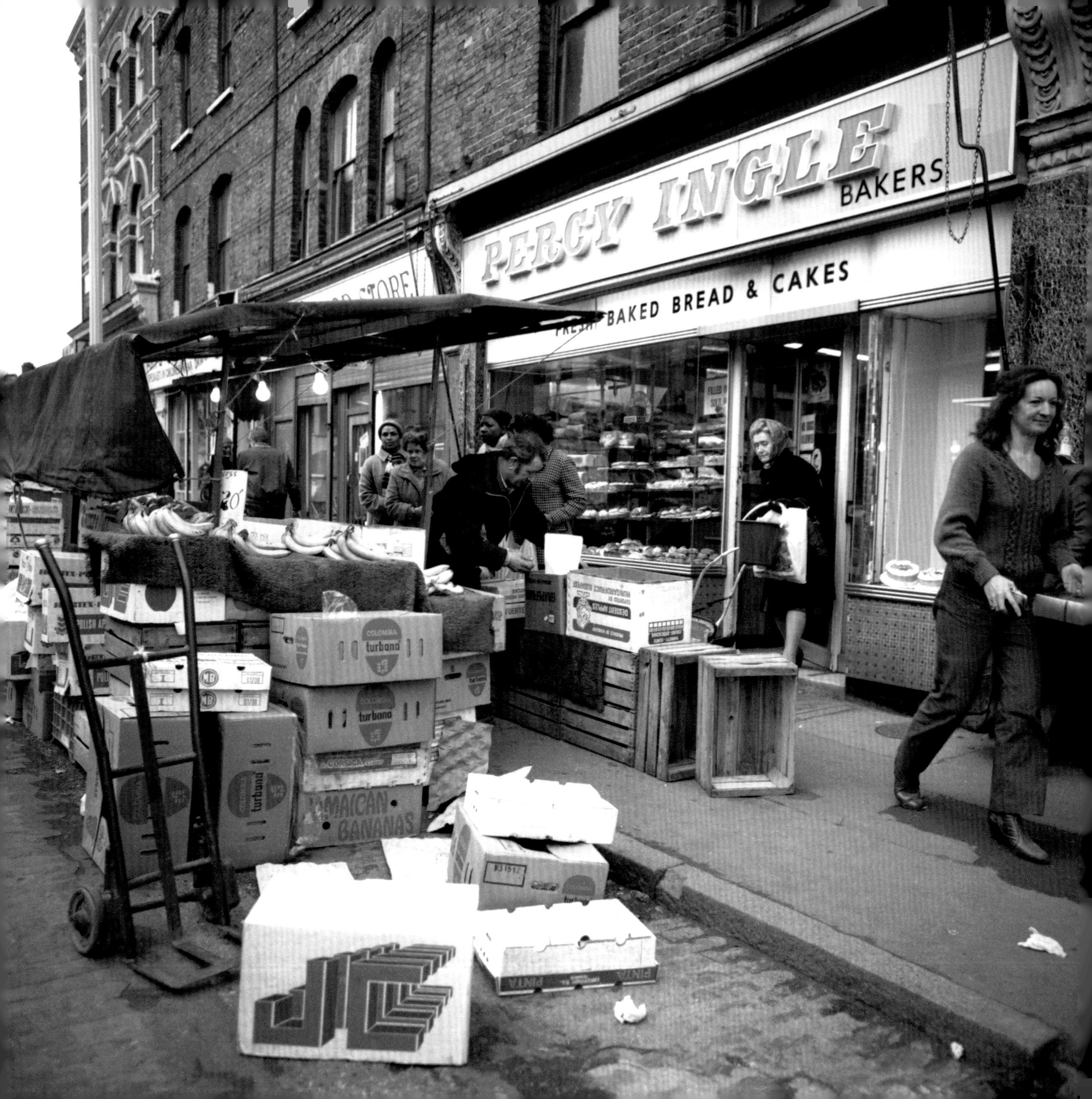

PERCY INGLE
BAKERS
FRESH BAKED BREAD & CAKES
COLOMBIA
turbana
JAMAICAN BANANAS
DESSERT APPLES

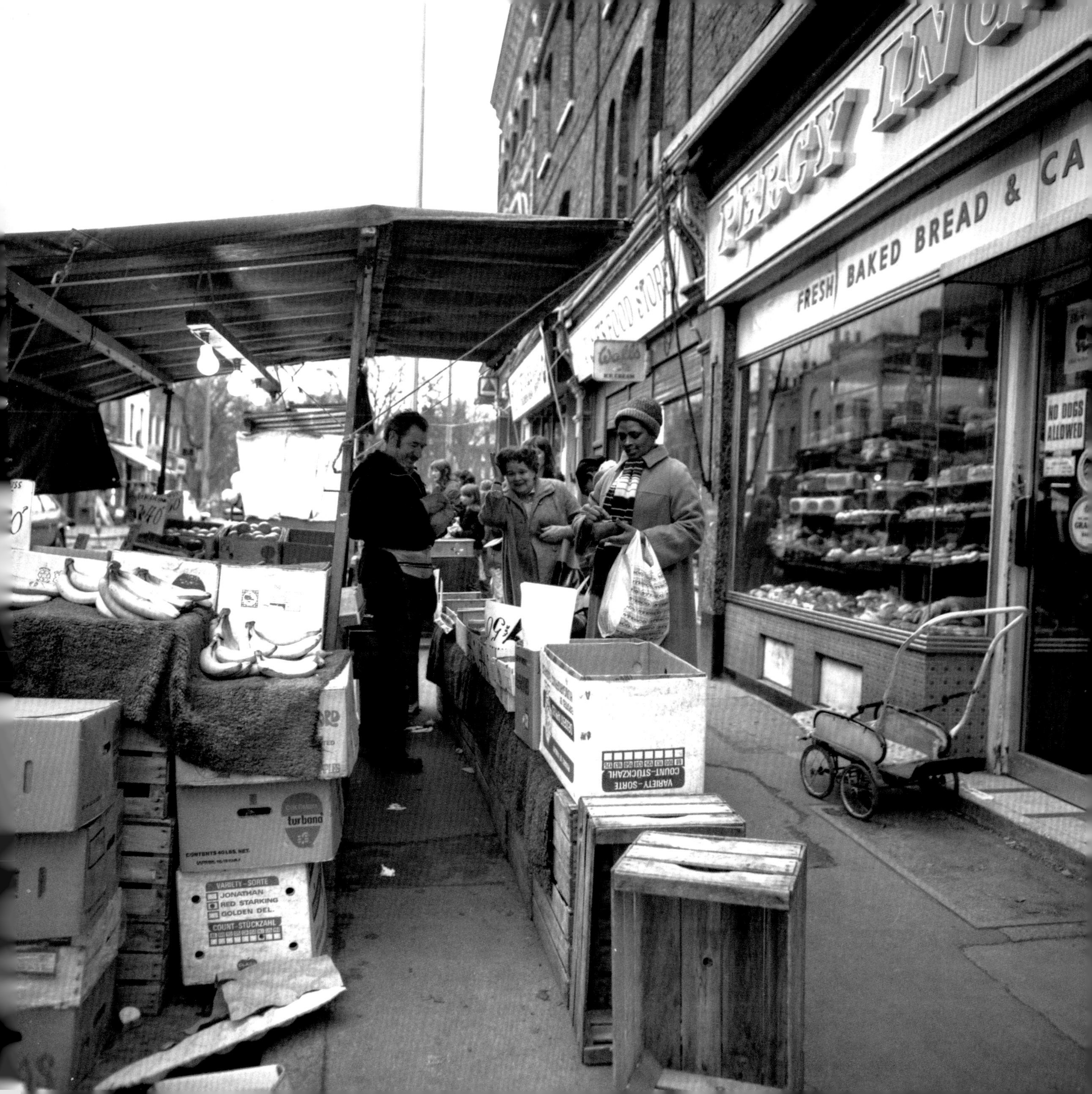

FRESH BAKED BREAD &
NO DOGS ALLOWED
VARIETY-SORTE
JONATHAN
RED STARKING
GOLDEN DEL.
COUNT-STÜCKZAHL
turbana
CONTENTS 40 LBS. NET

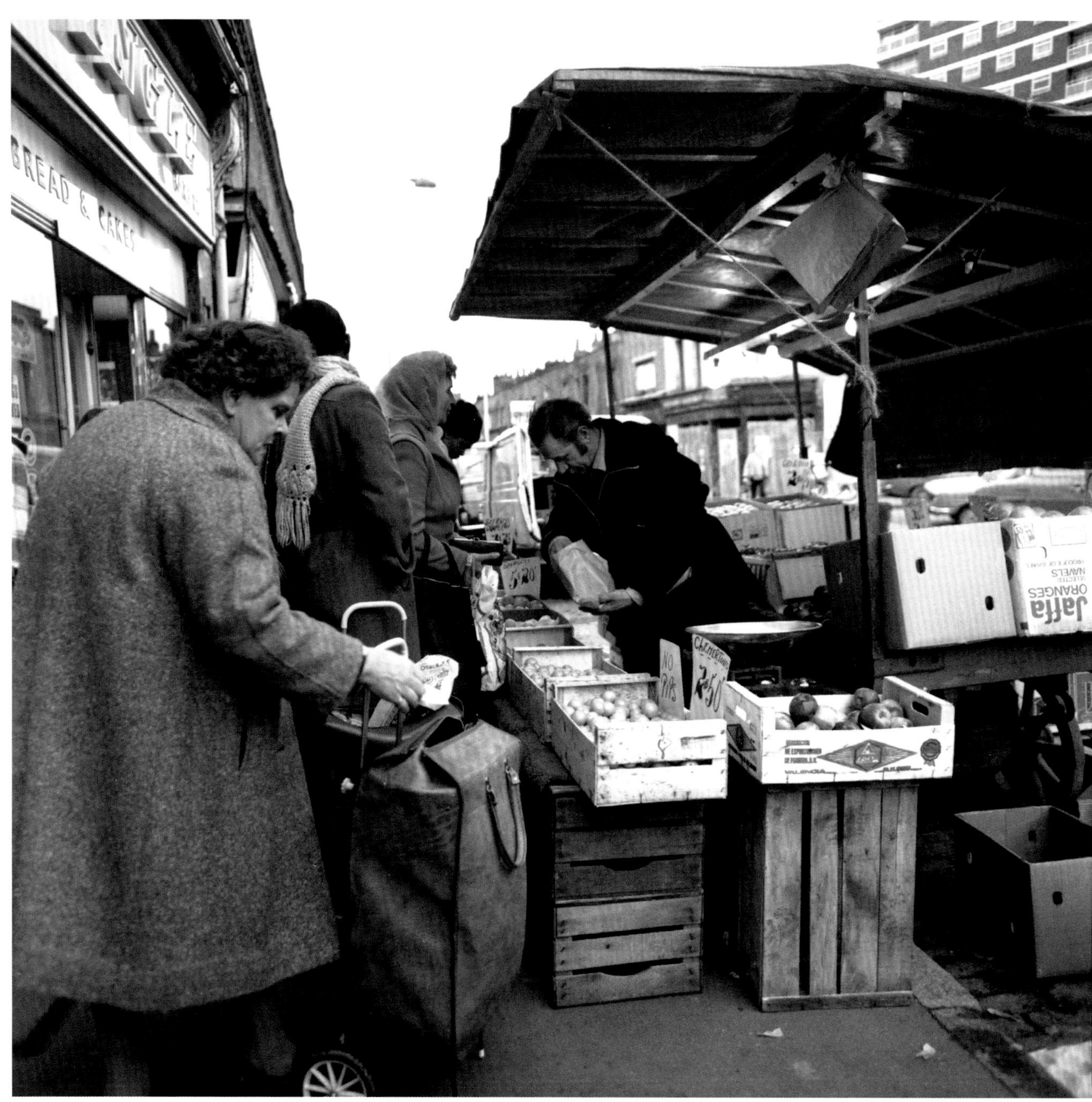
BREAD & CAKES
NO PIPS
Jaffa
ORANGES
NAVELS

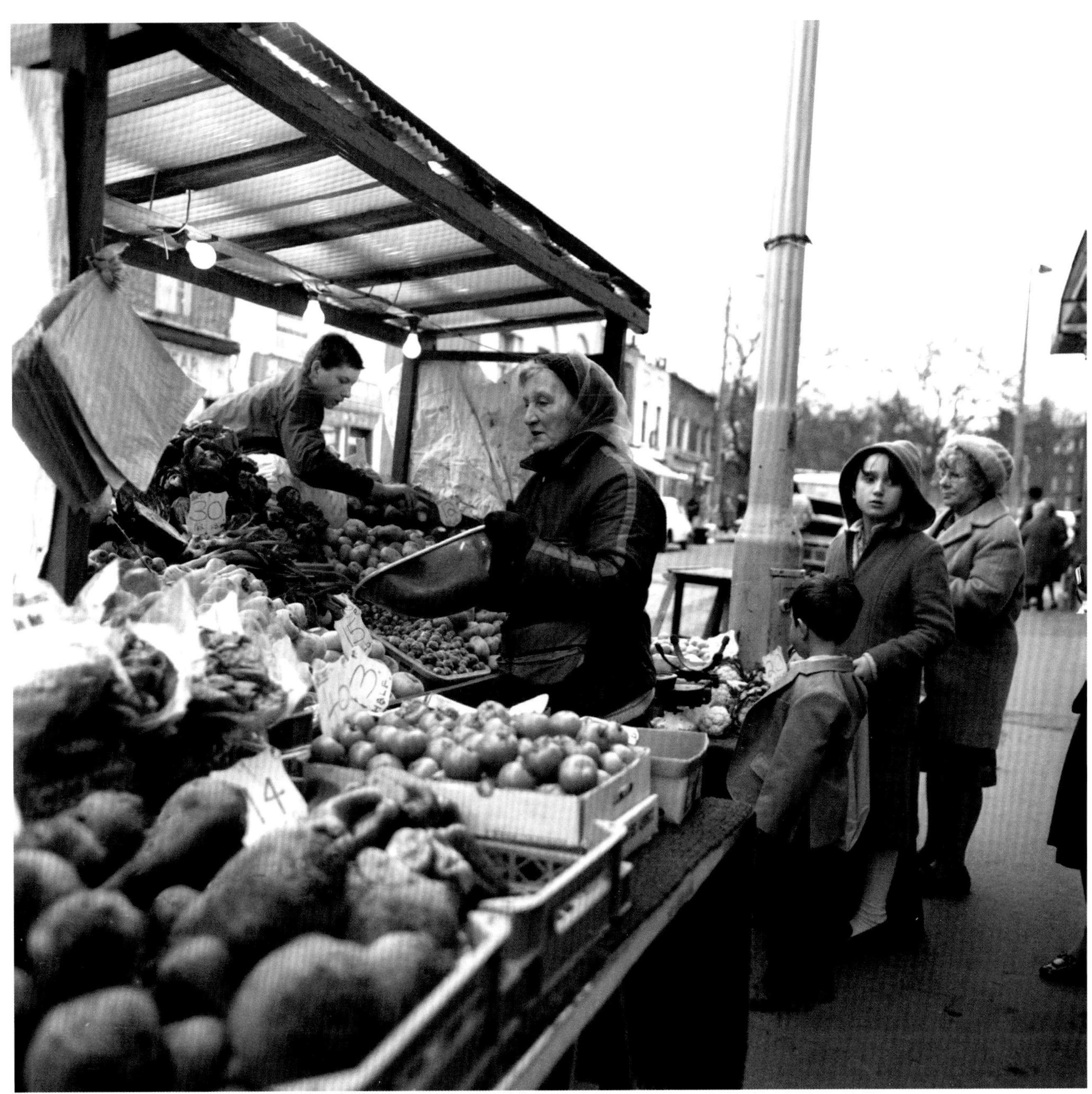
30
15
14

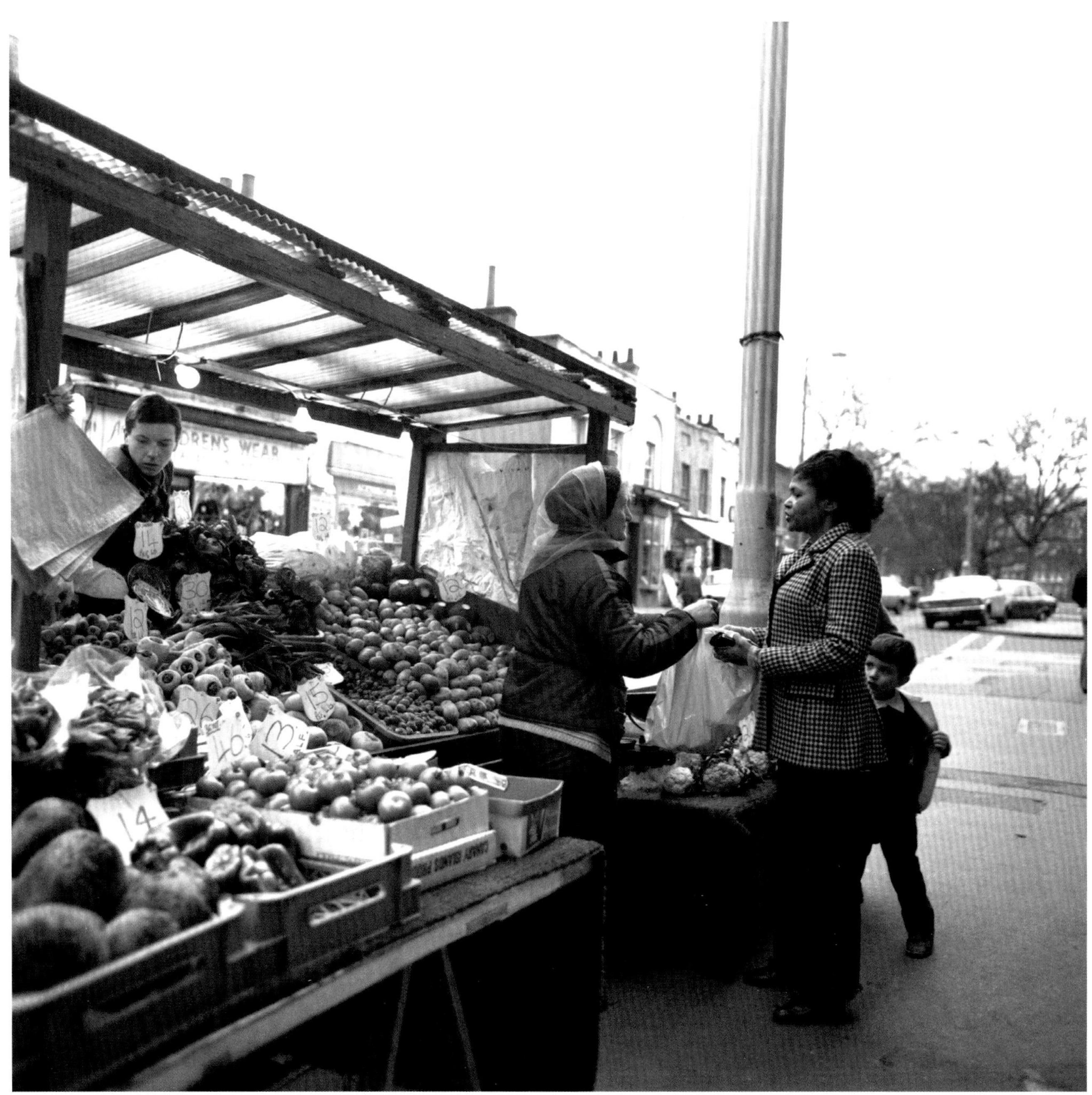
DRENS WEAR
14
30
13
14

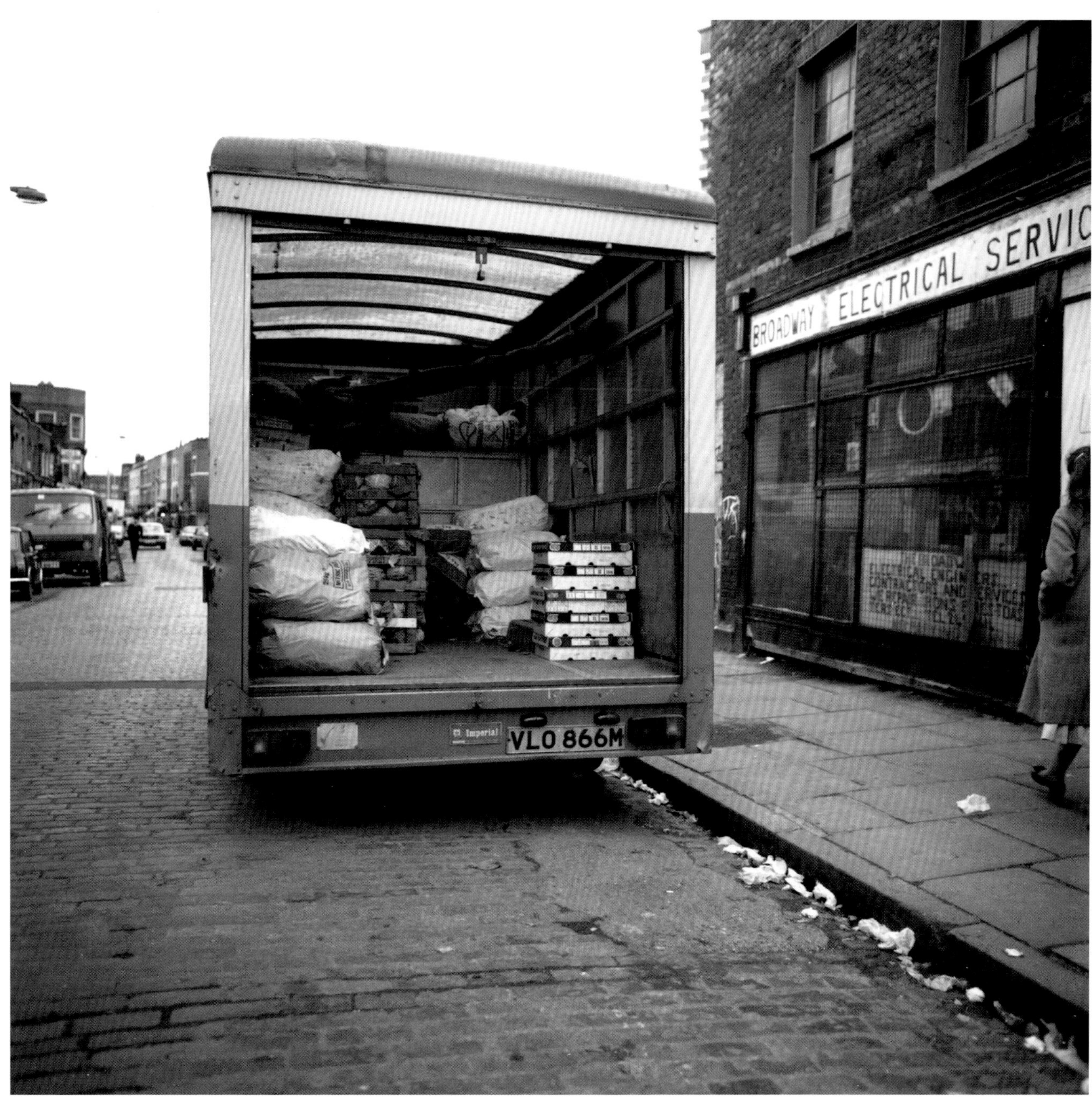
BROADWAY ELECTRICAL SERVIC
Imperial
VLO 866M

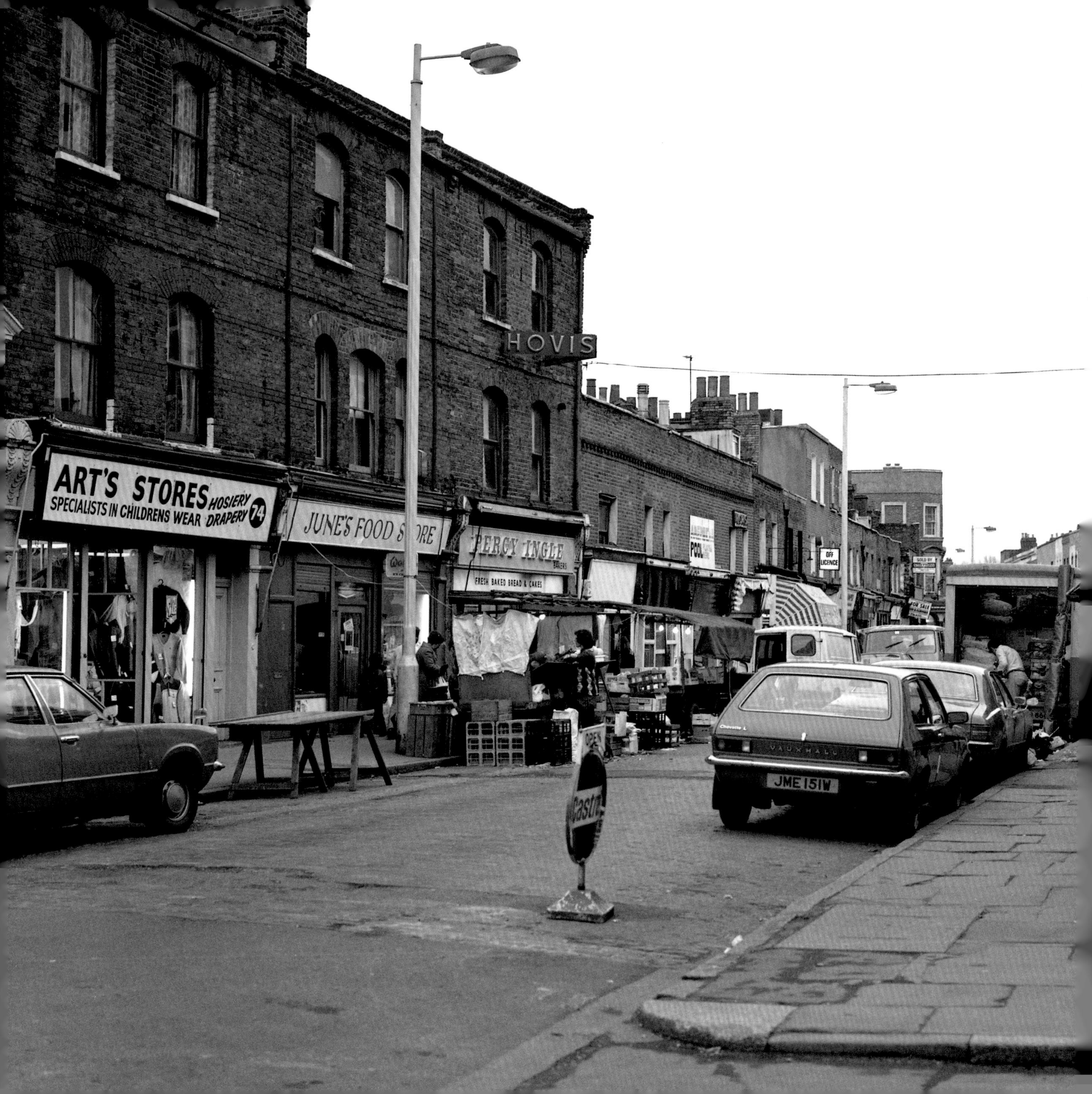
ART'S STORES
SPECIALISTS IN CHILDRENS WEAR
HOSIERY
DRAPERY
74
JUNE'S FOOD STORE
PERCY INGLE
BAKERS
FRESH BAKED BREAD & CAKES
HOVIS
POOL
OFF LICENCE
OPEN
JME 151W
VAUXHALL

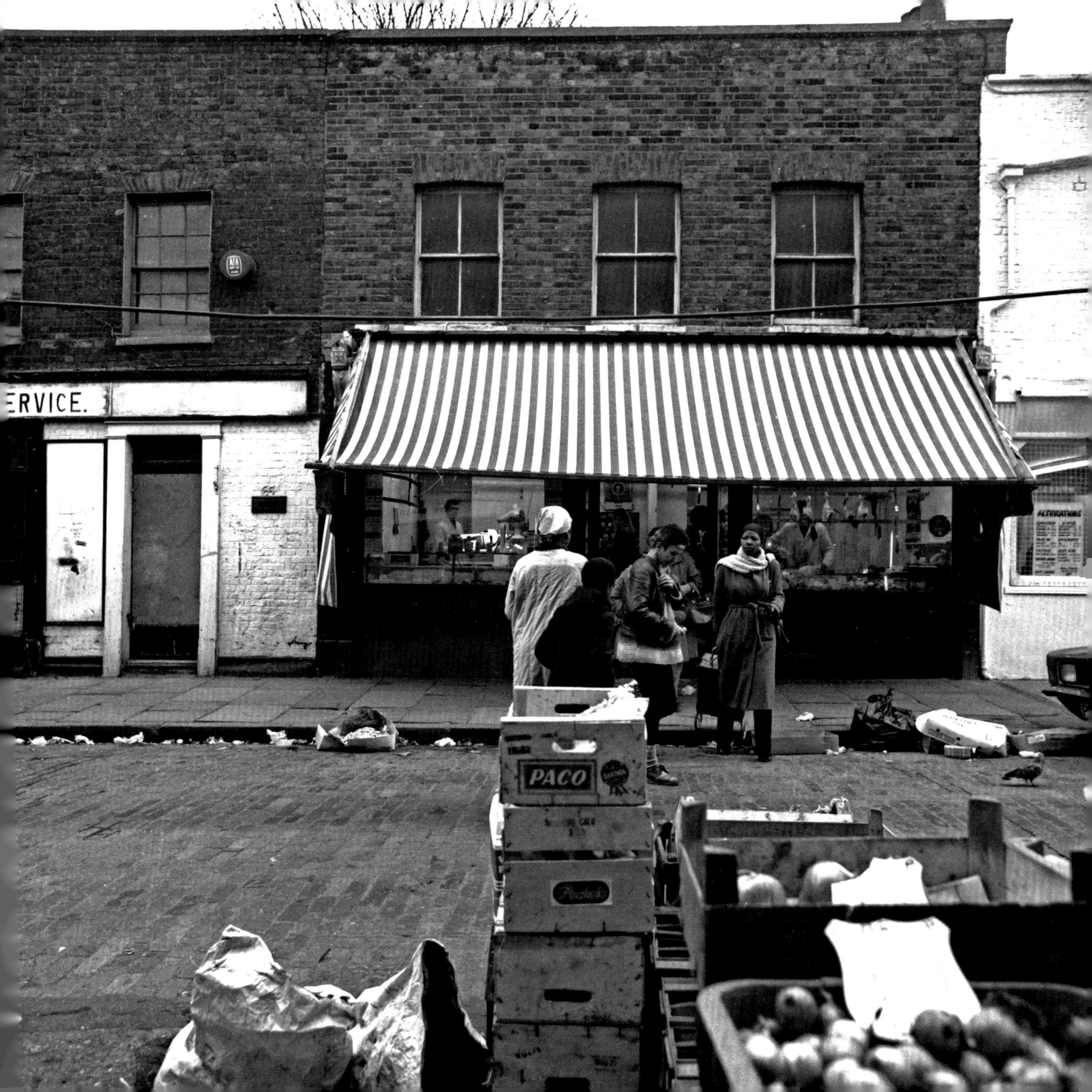
ERVICE.
ALTERATIONS
PACO

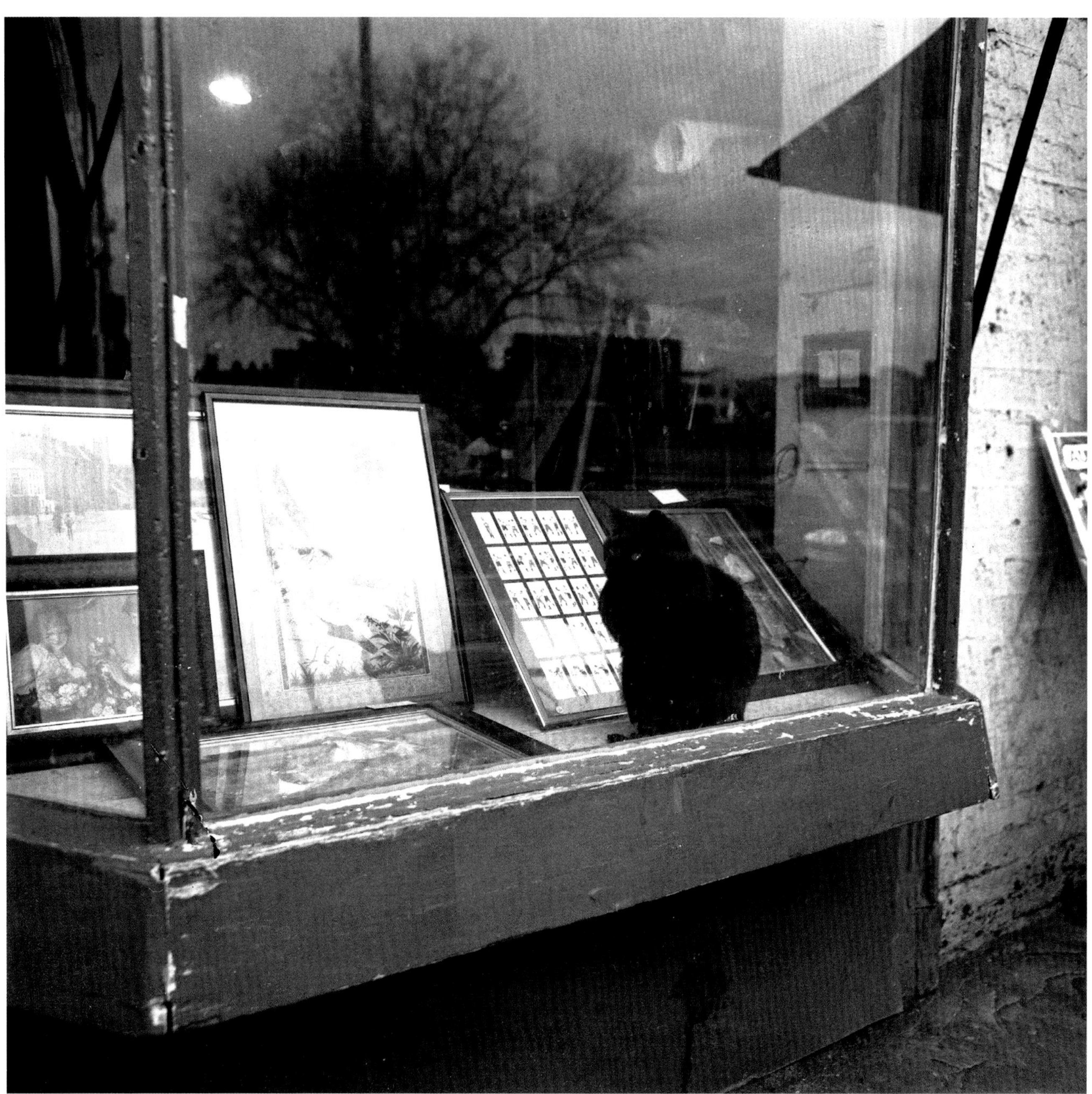

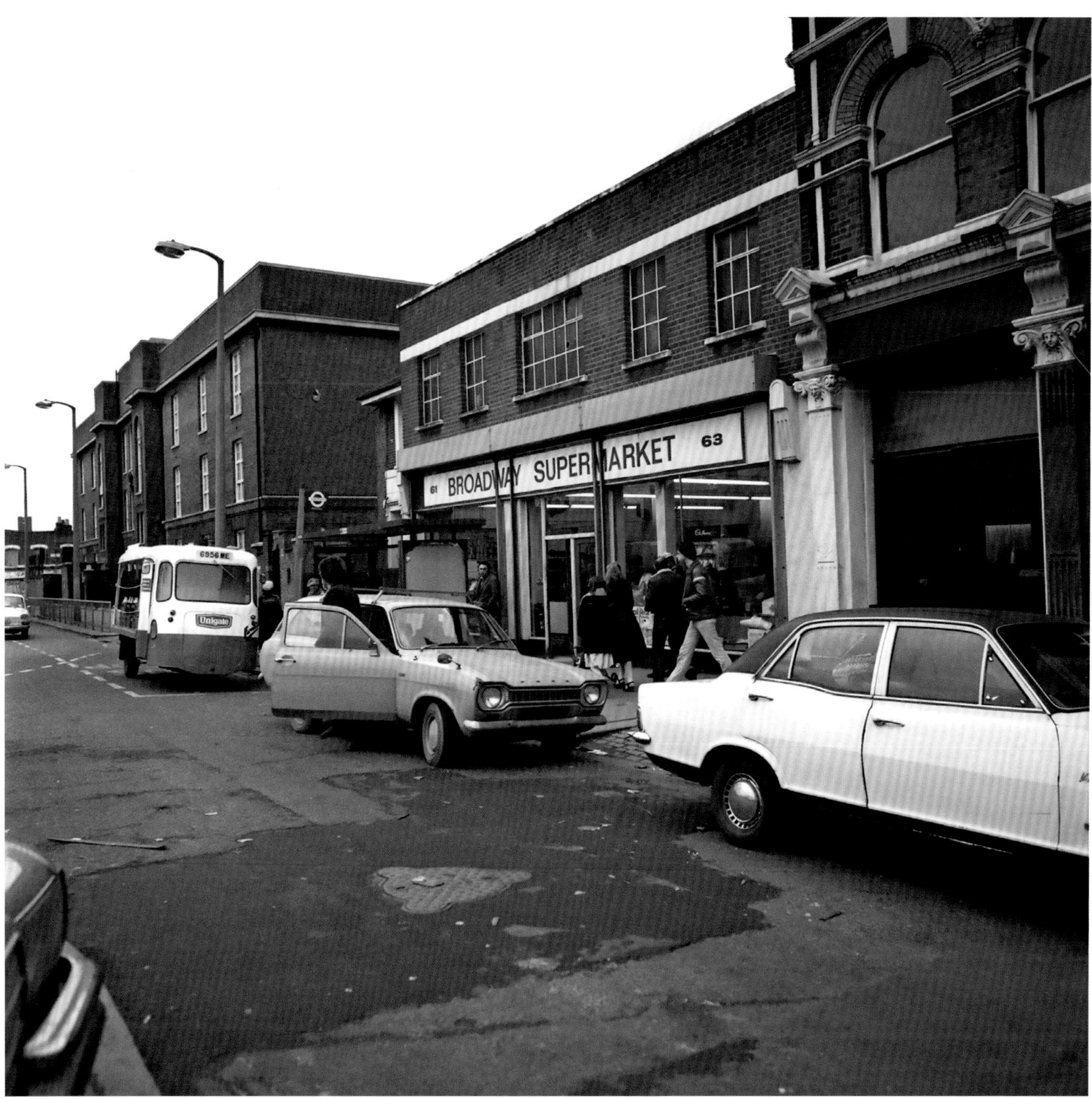
61 BROADWAY SUPERMARKET 63
Unigate

About Stuart Goodman

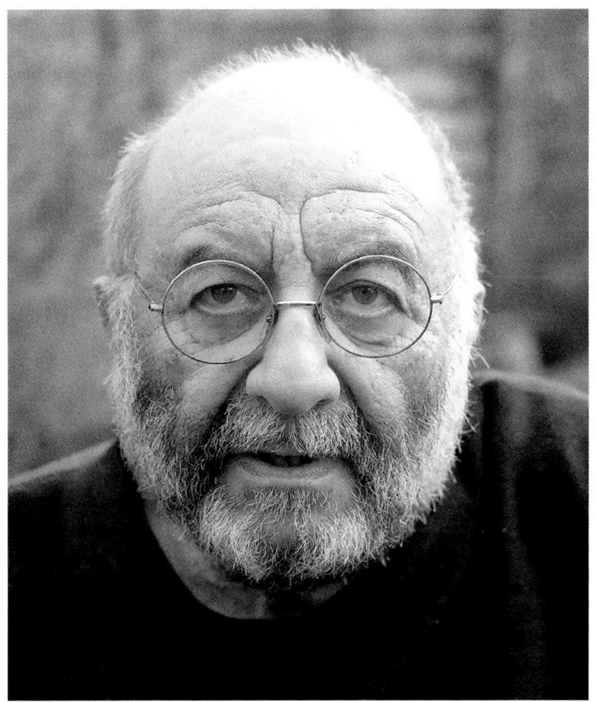

photo credit: Adam Goodman

Stuart Goodman, who at the time of publication is 72, was brought up on a council estate in Hackney. He survived a grammar school education, just, and went on to train, unsuccessfully, as a junior school teacher. He wanted to be a jazz trumpet player and played in the original National Youth Jazz Orchestra in the mid 1960s. His first national press publication was of NYJO at the Marquee club for the Times. The £4.12.6 fee changed his life.

He worked as a Fleet Street press snapper and picture editor for over twenty-five years. He and his wife Annie, a music therapist, now live in Norwich where he completed an M.A. in fine art, and taught photography at F.E. colleges and for adult education. He and Annie have two young people, Adam a photography graduate, and Joanna a community worker who acts as his responsible adult on occasion.

He and Adam opened an art gallery in Norwich, the Red Light Gallery, named of course after a darkroom safelight. The darkroom there included enlargers from the workshop of former Picture Post snapper Bert Hardy. The first images printed on them were these photographs of Broadway Market, after the negatives were rediscovered in Stuart's legendary filing system. They were later shown in the Off Broadway bar in the market where they were seen by Crystal and Jason of OWN IT!, the publisher of this book.

WWW.OWNIT.LONDON

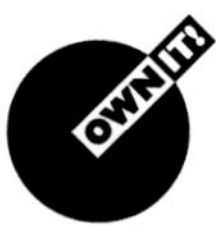